OVERCOMING SHYNESS

M. Blaine Smith

INTERVARSITY PRESS
DOWNERS GROVE, ILLINOIS 60515

InterVarsity Press® is the book-publishing division of InterVarsity Christian Fellowship®, a student movement active on campus at hundreds of universities, colleges and schools of nursing in the United States of America, and a member movement of the International Fellowship of Evangelical Students. For information about local and regional activities, write Public Relations Dept., InterVarsity Christian Fellowship, 6400 Schroeder Rd., P.O. Box 7895, Madison, WI 53707-7895.

All Scripture quotations, unless otherwise indicated, are taken from the HOLY BIBLE, NEW INTERNA-TIONAL VERSION®. NIV®. Copyright ©1973, 1978, 1984 by International Bible Society. Used by permission of Zondervan Publishing House. All rights reserved.

Cover photograph: Peter French

ISBN 0-8308-1630-5

Printed in the United States of America

Library of Congress Cataloging-in-Publication Data has been requested.

15	14	13	12	11	10	9	8	7	6	5	4	3	2	1
04	03	02	01	00	99	98	97	96	95	94	93			

Contents

Foreword

As a shy person myself, I found countless reasons for hope in *Overcoming Shyness*. Blaine points out some ways in which shyness is a gift, and yet he never trivializes the fears which so often immobilize shy people.

His biblical examples are eye-openers. How many of us have ever realized that so many of our favorite Bible heroes were hampered by shyness? And he gives contemporary examples of how biblical grace and affirmation have changed people whose lives had been wilted by shyness.

Blaine offers detailed, practical helps—always authentic, never gimmicky or artificial. All the shy people in the world owe Blaine Smith a tremendous debt of gratitude for writing *Overcoming Shyness*.

Steve Hayner
President, InterVarsity Christian Fellowship

Preface

My major concern in this book is to give help and encouragement to Christians who are chronically shy. Since I lived in those shoes for some time, my heart goes out to these people.

When our shyness is serious, it does not respond well to pep talks or spiritual platitudes. What we most need is positive experiences with people, experiences which build our confidence and help us outgrow our apprehensions. Yet we need a lot of help getting to that point, especially if in growing up we didn't have many of those successful experiences.

Usually our first need is to learn how to handle our fears. As we discover how to manage and live with the experience of fear itself, we gain the courage to take steps to become more outgoing. Typically, too, we need counsel on how to find the best opportunities for meeting people and advice on sharpening our interpersonal skills. On our own, we would just give up.

Often we need help in becoming more assertive. And without fail we have a pervasive need to develop a more optimistic outlook, to break with our habit of always expecting the worst; we need solid suggestions on how to do this.

In the chapters ahead I will give careful attention to each of these areas and offer as much practical advice as I possibly can.

Part two focuses on handling our fears, part three on improving our social opportunities and skills, and part four on learning to be assertive and optimistic.

First, though, it will help to devote several chapters to looking more closely at the origins of shyness (chapter two) and the effect it has upon our life (chapters three and four). We will note in chapter three that there are actually some surprising benefits to being shy! These can stay with us even as we become more outgoing, and appreciating them helps us gain the incentive to change.

I am also including an appendix with suggestions for handling public speaking and performance situations.

While my primary aim is to help the chronically shy Christian, many of the topics in the book are also pertinent to those who are less seriously shy or who need help in a specific area. Please feel free to scan the table of contents and pick out those portions which will most benefit you. If you are looking to this book for help in overcoming deep-seated shyness, though, I do recommend reading the chapters in sequence. They are designed to help you gain a foothold step by step, and each chapter provides some foundation for the ones that follow.

No matter how extreme your shyness is, I am certain its impact in your life can be substantially reduced. My own experience and that of many other Christians convince me of this. *You can overcome the unhealthy effects of shyness without losing the benefits it provides and without violating the personality God has given you.*

The Scriptures, especially, convince me that Christ brings significant healing of shyness—when we take those steps which allow us to cooperate fully with his grace. This book is dedicated to helping you do that. May the Lord bless you richly and give you every success as you move ahead.

Part One

Understanding Shyness

Chapter One

A Common Experience

It was the most terrifying experience of my life. It took me most of the school year to get up my resolve to do it. Finally, on a Sunday evening in February, I sat down by the phone, an older friend at my side coaxing me on. My friend gave me many convincing reasons why I should make the call, and I agreed with them all. I simply could not do it.

I actually picked up the phone. I began to dial the number . . . then quickly hung up. I tried again. "Go ahead!" my friend said. I tried *again*.

As the evening wore on, it became evident that my fingers simply lacked the capacity to dial this number. Besides, it was too late now. I gave up, both discouraged and relieved.

For the next two evenings I was back repeating the ritual. For several hours I tried—and occasionally succeeded in dialing the entire number. But the receiver button still won out before the first ring. I was finding that it can be a long way from the intellect to the emotions and will.

Wednesday night had a sense of now or never. If I waited any longer it would be too late in the week. With all my heart and soul I wanted to make the call. Finally, after numerous aborted tries, I completed the number. Before I could stop it, the call connected and the first ring sounded. I held on. The second came. The third was abruptly halted as someone picked up the receiver. Her father answered, and I asked if she was home. Now I was fully committed. I wondered if I would faint.

After a thirty-second eternity she picked up the phone, and I managed to identify myself.

"Blaine!" she exclaimed with the exhilaration of a mother finding a lost child. I could scarcely believe that she was this happy to hear from me.

Timidly I let out the long-rehearsed question, "Would you, uh, like to go to the movies with me Saturday night?"

"Really?" she shouted back with even greater excitement. The ice was now well broken.

A Real Battle

As I reflect on my first experience of asking a girl out for a date as a young teenager, I'm struck by how many of the thoughts that accompanied my shyness were utterly irrational. For months I had been plagued with fears that she would reject me, belittle me, laugh at me if I broached the question of getting together. Yet if I had never taken that painful step of phoning her, these fears would never have been shown to be the straw men which they were. No amount of philosophizing, no amount of encouragement from someone else could substitute for that existential moment of taking the initiative.

The experience in many ways is a parable for my life. Until my early twenties I fought with shyness, and at times it immobilized me. To this day it bothers me at times. But when I have taken decided action to break out of its inertia, the results have usually been wonderfully surprising. Not that I've always received the kind of response I did on that phone call, and not that I haven't experienced hurt at times. But the results of conquering shyness have usually been far superior to being paralyzed by it.

Yet I remember too well how I came within a hair's breadth of not making the call. Were it not for the encouragement of my older friend, I seriously doubt I'd have done it. For so many shy persons the step is never taken. The receiver button forever wins. And with each thwarted attempt fears are magnified and the barrier of shyness becomes greater to cross.

Widespread and Universal

Whether or not you consider yourself a shy person, you may be surprised to know how many in our society actually do. Psychologist Philip Zimbardo, as part of a monumental study of shyness, surveyed nearly 5,000 people. He reports his results:

> The most basic finding of our research establishes that shyness is common, widespread, and universal. More than 80 percent of those questioned reported that they were shy at some point in their lives, either now, in the past, or always. Of these, over 40 percent considered themselves *presently shy*—that means four out of every ten people you meet, or 84 million Americans! . . . To say shyness is a universal experience is a rather broad generalization, but one with a solid basis. Only about 7 percent of all Americans sampled reported that they have never, ever experienced feelings of shyness. Similarly, in other cultures, only a small minority of people claim to have never personally experienced shyness.[1]

We may define shyness as an exaggerated fear of rejection or negative response from others. Usually, too, it is a fear which is *inhibiting* in its effect—it holds us back from doing things we want to do. This does not mean that all who are shy are fearful in every type of social encounter. Many people experience shyness in some areas but not others. There are many who find it perfectly natural to make friends—even with members of the opposite sex—yet are traumatized at broaching any sort of dating relationship. Others are uncomfortable initiating *any* opposite-sex friendship.

Well before my unnerving episode of making the phone call I had learned to be comfortable performing music before an audience. For some reason stage fright was not a problem for me when performing. I felt at home standing in front of several hundred people with the guitar but panic-stricken at the thought of striking up a relationship with just one person.

I have known others who suffer from the opposite extreme. Kathy, a college friend, is quite at ease in personal relationships and goes out of her way in church fellowship meetings to help others feel welcome. But she is terrified to sing in front of even a small audience, in spite of her exceptional vocal talent. (Again I confess the irony in my own life, for while I am not usually prone to stage fright in musical performing, I am in public speaking.)

For some, the greatest problem with shyness comes in seeking a job or advancement within their profession. There is great embarrassment in speaking to others about their gifts and potential. They feel morbidly self-seeking to raise the question of salary or job benefits. It can be especially difficult for women seeking opportunities in professional areas dominated by men. And in spite of the advances of the last several decades, women still have to contend with the stereotype that being assertive is not compatible with being feminine. Not a few women feel uncomfortable seeking any career improvement.

Yet men, too, often feel awkward speaking up about their qualifications or salary needs. If women do have a greater struggle in this area than men, there is no evidence that women in general are more inclined to be shy. In fact, Zimbardo notes just the opposite: In a survey of college students, more men than women reported being shy.[2]

When Fear Paralyzes
Some apprehension in beginning a friendship or coming into a

new situation is normal. Indeed, to experience anxiety at such times can be healthy, for it makes us more alert, more responsive to another's needs, more effective in our work. But for shy persons the anxiety is excessive. Fears are greatly exaggerated, to the point where they immobilize us. Shy people are often intelligent, creative individuals with highly active imaginations. Their minds work overtime manufacturing imagined catastrophes which seldom occur.

When a person comes to faith in Christ, this same capacity for mental depth can lend itself to a vibrant faith which is a great antidote to shyness. But shyness can also pose a barrier to faith. God has promised indescribable blessings to the Christian. There are relationships, opportunities for investing our gifts, and experiences of growth for each of us which are nothing short of extraordinary. *Yet it takes steps of faith to come into these blessings,* and a step of faith means going forward in spite of less than perfect certainty about the outcome. Shy people are so prone to imagine disaster that they may be frightened to take that step of faith—and even convince themselves that God doesn't want them to.

When I look honestly at my own experience as a shy teenager, I think that my greatest fears were not over the other person's reaction but over my own. *Will I make an idiot of myself if I strike up a conversation? Will I clam up and not be able to speak? Will I pass out?* Very often this is the essence of the problem for the shy person. Again Philip Zimbardo comments:

Most of us have occasion to blush, feel our hearts pounding, or find "butterflies" in our stomachs. Not-shy people accept these reactions as mild discomfort and look to the positive aspects of what might happen later—having a good conversation with the minister at the church social, getting the right directions from a French gendarme, learning the latest dance step. Shy people, however, tend to *concentrate* on these physical symptoms. In fact, sometimes they don't even wait to get into a situation that might make them feel shy. They experience the symptoms in advance, and thinking only of disaster, decide to avoid the church social or the tour to Paris or the dance.[3]

Introverts and Extroverts

In noting what shyness is, we also need to point out what it is not. Many assume that being shy is the same as being introverted. While introverts are sometimes shy, shyness and introversion are not the same, nor do they always occur together. Introverts are people who, to put it simply, *enjoy* being alone. They treasure time alone above time with people. They may be very good in relating with people; they may be lots of fun. But too much time socializing can exhaust them, not because they are frightened of people but because of their inherent need for solitude.

A friend of mine, Sylvia, is a thirty-nine-year-old homemaker. She explains it this way: "I need time alone or I get frazzled: I have a 'privacy tank' that has to be watched."

Larry, a forty-five-year-old pastor friend, describes his introversion: "My world is within me. I derive energy from within. People drain me, though I enjoy people. My best work is done through reflection rather than action. I think first and may act later."

Sylvia and Larry are both energized by being alone, and this is characteristic of the introvert. Their need for solitude is healthy, for it is part of the personality mix God has given them. Because introverts are not as motivated to seek out people as extroverts are, though, they typically have less social experience while growing up. The result is that many introverts do become shy. Their lack of involvement with people keeps them from the sort of experience needed to gain social confidence, and their time alone gives more opportunity for a fear of people to fester.

It does not have to work this way, though. Introverts who have the good fortune of being raised in an affirming atmosphere where others are outgoing toward them may develop strong social confidence. There is nothing about the personality trait of introversion which *requires* one to become shy.

While Moses is a classic example in Scripture of a shy introvert, Jacob appears to be an introvert who was not shy. That he was an introvert seems clear enough—Genesis describes him as "a quiet man" (Gen 25:27). But when we study Jacob's life, we find no evidence he was shy. When he fell in love with Rebecca, for instance, he was highly assertive about his desire to marry her. He was even crafty and aggressive and did whatever it took to accomplish his goals.

While it is true that the introvert is not always shy, it is just as true that the extrovert is not always as brimming over with social confidence as we might suppose. Extroverts are energized by being with people. They become listless, bored or tired if isolated from social contact for very long. But the fact that they are motivated to socialize does not mean they are necessarily comfortable doing so. If while growing up they do not have positive experiences with people to build their confidence, they may develop the fears typical of shyness.

Enlightening Examples

A thirty-five-year-old friend of mine, Dessia, was excessively shy until her late twenties. Her parents were so verbally abusive of her that she kept quiet most of the time to keep from inflaming them. She was sick for much of her childhood, so she had little interaction with her peers, and she became chronically fearful of initiating contact with others. She describes her life as "filled with shyness, fear and sadness."

At age twenty-nine, though, she began seeing a Christian counselor who helped her considerably. The self-understanding which emerged was intriguing. "I actually found out that my basic personality is very extroverted," she explains. "I get my energy from people. Before, I thought I was introverted—but after seeing that my shyness was just a tool to protect myself from being hurt, I was able to learn new skills and let my real personality out. I always felt there was this really neat person trapped inside of me, inside bars of fear and pain. I still have a lot of work to do on these fears, but I feel like the 'real me' is expressing itself, and I feel so much happier."

Dessia's experience illustrates how one can be an extrovert by nature yet—for any of a number of reasons—still be shy. This pattern is actually quite common. I suspect, in fact, that there are as many extroverts in the body of Christ who are shy as there are introverts.

One of these is Dr. Steve Hayner. Dr. Hayner, who is president of InterVarsity Christian Fellowship, publicly describes himself as a "shy extrovert." In an interview for this book he told me, "I am energized by interaction with people far more than by time alone." Yet he also spoke of a lifelong battle with shyness and graphically described different situations which have been difficult for him. One of these is shopping:

"Until five years ago, I never liked shopping. I didn't want to deal with store clerks if I didn't know them. When I needed to buy clothes, I would usually do it in my home town where I grew up, even though I hadn't lived there for years. There was one store where I knew the owners. So I'd wait to shop until I was home visiting my parents! And until recent years it just about paralyzed me to ask a stranger for directions or for any advice at all. So there's been a lot of fear associated with these things."

Hayner went on to say that his uneasiness approaching strangers extended to Christian fellowship situations as well:

"At the University Presbyterian Church in Seattle where I first served as a pastor, the ministers made a practice before the Sunday service of walking up and down the aisles shaking hands. Most people absolutely loved it. But for me it was just horrible— the worst part of my week. The idea of taking the initiative with people I didn't know in that kind of context was very, very difficult. This despite the fact that I was interacting with students and people throughout the week."

Hayner's gracious honesty in sharing his experience brings out just how strongly someone in leadership can suffer from shyness fears which we might assume trouble only the socially isolated. His testimony is especially interesting, for he is greatly loved and respected as he directs a large parachurch ministry. Being an extrovert—even a very successful one—does not shield one from the possibility of being shy. Nor does shyness have to be allowed to control one's life and prevent successful relationships.

A number of biblical characters appear to me to be shy extroverts, including the apostle Peter, Esther, King Saul, and Mary, Jesus' mother. Saul, for instance, sometimes demonstrated the extreme fears which are typical of chronic shyness. When Samuel was to present him to the Israelites as king, Saul hid himself among the baggage (1 Sam 10:22). Yet in the company of outgoing people he rallied and came alive. Thus, on occasions when he met a band of prophets, he quickly joined in their exuberant activity (1 Sam 10:10-12; 19:23-24).

Shyness and Phobias

It becomes easier to understand how someone unlikely can be shy, when we realize that shyness in its extreme form is actually a phobia. A phobia by definition is an illogical fear that is way out of line with any true risks involved. It does not disappear simply because we recognize it is irrational. Others may give us a mountain of evidence that our fear is unfounded—and we may agree. Still, we are afraid. Understanding shyness as a phobia helps us appreciate why it can be so intractable.

Phobia is also the best word we have to underscore the debilitating nature of serious shyness. When we listen to the testimonies of chronically shy people, it becomes clear that no other word adequately depicts their plight. Here is how some shy Christians have described their ordeals to me:

☐ "I can't look people in the eye. I get sick inside, even have pain. I can't enjoy the company of others or gain from their experiences. I feel like there is a tight band around my brain, like it cuts all the blood off when I am with people, and reason goes out the window. My mind knows I am in no danger but my heart will not believe. It makes me regret being alive."

□ "My shyness is a definite hindrance—especially as I pursue a career in ministry! I find myself often to be intimidated and fearful in group situations. Public speaking is at times very painful—but I push myself and do it anyway."

□ "Shyness to me feels like being put in an airtight glass container. I feel isolated, yet people can look at me. At times I feel as if I'm smothering. I feel sometimes as if I'm missing out on a lot because of my fear of others."

□ "Shyness can be frightening—it makes me feel very self-conscious and alone and isolated. It also makes me feel very awkward and ill-at-ease. Even when I manage to cover up the external shyness, on the inside I am very nervous."

□ "My shyness inhibits me to the extreme at times. I find myself *wanting* to talk with people, to get to know people, but my mind goes blank. I can't think of things to talk about or ask, and I'm unable to start a conversation even if I do have something to say. The silence becomes overwhelming. It's devastating!"

□ "Shyness has caused many, many moments of pain and anxiety in my life. For the most part it can hold you prisoner to things you want to do and say but are afraid to."

These individuals are speaking of a level of shyness that is clearly phobic in nature. It robs them of joy and hinders them from taking steps they would like to take. This is not to suggest that shyness is always this paralyzing for everyone. Many who call themselves shy are only mildly nervous about certain social situations and usually manage to get beyond their inhibitions. But for countless people, shyness is a chronic problem and a constant drag upon their lives. *Phobia* is not too strong a word to describe it.

A Reason for Hope

If terming shyness a phobia highlights how debilitating it can be, it also gives us a reason for hope, for *phobias can be overcome.* There are steps which are always effective in lessening the grip of phobic fear, and there's much that can be done to conquer the inhibitions of shyness itself. I know many Christians who have made considerable strides in overcoming shyness, and I write this book with the strong conviction that each of us *can* gain greater confidence and effectiveness with people. With this as a goal, let's move ahead.

Chapter Two

The Roots of Shyness

We who are shy are intensely curious to know how we got this way. Were we born shy? Did we inherit the condition? Are there factors in our background which caused it? Did we catch it like a virus from a passerby? Or is it merely a bad habit that needs to be broken?

In reality, shyness can come about in lots of ways and for lots of reasons. When we compare experiences as shy people, it is intriguing to find just how different our backgrounds have often been. There is no one influence which in itself guarantees one will become shy. When we look closely at our past, we usually find several important factors that have contributed.

There are benefits, though, to making the effort to understand the roots of our own shyness. For one thing, knowing *how we got to where we are* helps us better see *where to go from here*. Different causes of shyness suggest different routes to healing. If my shyness springs mainly from certain bad habits of thinking and is not deep-seated, I may simply need to work on developing a more optimistic outlook. But if a difficult family background is involved, then counseling may help me to come to terms with past wounds.

Understanding why we are shy also helps us avoid behavior that might induce shyness in others. We who are shy too often influence our children to become so, and sometimes others as well. If we can identify ways in which people's attitudes have hurt us, we can avoid repeating the pattern in our relationships with others.

In addition, simply understanding the causes of shyness frees us from any fatalistic notion that it is an indelible trait which we can do nothing to change. Some fear their shyness is a genetic or inherent condition which must be with them for life. While genetics may sometimes play a minor role in shyness, the major cause is always factors in our life experience. Knowing this frees us to look honestly at what we can do to counteract the influence of these factors. It gives us hope that we can improve.

Are We Born Shy?
There is an increasing tendency in some circles to suggest that shyness may have a genetic or biological link. Though the idea is not widespread, it is expressed occasionally in articles and in books such as David Sheehan's *The Anxiety Disease*[1] and Anne Moir's *Brain Sex*.[2] This idea usually fails to have a redemptive effect on the shy person. We who are shy are such creatures of suggestion that simply hearing our shyness might be genetically based leads us to worry that our condition is either hopeless or only treatable through medicine. Indeed, the very thought that there could be a biological basis for our condition makes us panicky.

The evidence fails to convince me, though, that the biological link is all that clear. It is well established that certain chemical imbalances in the brain can make a person prone to anxiety and panic attacks. But if chemical imbalance were the primary cause of one's fear, panic would occur unpredictably and would not be associated with only one type of fearful situation. We who are shy are frightened of certain encounters with people. Our fear is *focused* and related to this specific area, even though we may be quite comfortable or even courageous in other situations. This suggests that our fear is a learned response and not triggered by biological factors. In this case our shyness fits the classic definition of a phobia.

If, in addition to being shy, you are prey to frequent flashes of panic which do not seem associated with any frightening situation, then a chemical imbalance may be at fault. Fortunately this problem can almost always be successfully treated medically. See a physician or psychiatrist and ask for help. There is no shame in doing this, any more than there is in asking for any other type of medical assistance. Keep in mind, though, that *consistent* fear of social situations also suggests that you have some learned fear in addition to the chemical problem. It will still help to follow the steps suggested in this book for dealing specifically with your shyness.

If your fear is mainly related to certain types of encounters with people, rest assured a chemical imbalance is not the culprit. Your shyness results from factors in your background, patterns of thinking you have learned, or both. You are shy in the conventional sense. Your shyness is an *acquired* fear—and thus it can be "unacquired" (gotten rid of) as well.

But what about the personality factor? Can we be born with a temperament which is inherently shy? I find no evidence this is ever true. Certain factors in our personality, such as being introverted or nonaggressive, may cause others to treat us in ways that sow the seeds of shyness. But these personality factors are not the same as being shy, and they do not ensure that we will become shy. If we are raised in an affirming environment where our distinctiveness and gifts are appreciated, then we may acquire strong confidence with people in spite of our quiet nature.

By the same token, an analytical personality can make us

vulnerable to being shy, for it may incline us to worry obsessively about how others will respond to us. But this does not have to happen. Our obsessing may be directed toward areas other than social encounters. And many analytical people learn to harness their mental energy for optimistic thinking. An analytical personality does not require that one become a ruminator.

All of this is good news for those of us who are shy, for it suggests that there is *always* something we can do to overcome the unhealthy effects of shyness. We are not bound to this condition in the way we are to a chronic allergy. We can take steps to break free of our inhibitions.

Knowing this, let's look at the factors which do have critical bearing on whether one becomes shy. Family background is often a major influence.

The Effects of Family Background

Recently I included a "Shyness Survey" with my newsletter, giving readers who have struggled with shyness a chance to share their experiences and insights with me. Over a hundred were quickly returned, many filled out in considerable detail. One of the questions I asked on the survey was, "Do you feel your shyness is related to factors in your upbringing? Can you identify them?" Only four individuals stated that they saw no connection between their upbringing and being shy. Most felt their shyness resulted in part from how they were treated by family members while growing up. Experiences vary widely though, and I find there are five types of family backgrounds which often foster shyness.

1. The unaffirming family. About half the survey respondents note that their family background was not an affirming one. Some speak of outright physical or sexual abuse. Others simply say that praise from family members was minimal or nonexistent. Many refer to their family environment as overly strict, repressive, and one in which mistakes and imperfections were not tolerated. The testimonies are most revealing:

☐ "There were five children in our family. My father didn't like noise, so he would tell us often to be quiet. At the dinner table if the radio was on and he wanted to hear something in particular while we were talking, he would tell us to be silent. So I grew up pretty much keeping a lot inside."

☐ "I was teased a lot by my brothers and grew to believe what they said."

☐ "My father used a lot of physical punishment to discipline me. There was no consistent affirmation of him loving me, such as hugs or words like 'I love you.' My mother would push me away when I tried to hug her and crawl into her lap."

☐ "My father never listened—just talked at me."

☐ "Because I was yelled at frequently by my mother, I learned not to say anything or do anything that would upset her."

☐ "I was told growing up that I was a mistake, and I was never wanted. Also, that I would never amount to anything. Many different statements like this were said to me throughout my childhood. Also, my parents never really talked to me, not at length. I guess you could basically say that I feared people wouldn't like me—so why bother trying to talk to them?"

☐ "I was always being put down by my parents—for example, they said, 'Walk five yards behind me so no one will know we are together.' "

☐ "My father is an archetypal extrovert—loud, opinionated, aggressive, angry. His opinion was always the most important one in the household. The family has tended to pivot around placating my father and protecting my mother from noise, worry and any other of life's problems."

☐ "Being told one should mind one's own business made me feel people are unapproachable. I was not encouraged to participate in conversation when adult friends were visiting but was given the sense that children should be seen, not heard."

☐ "Both parents drank a lot and our needs as children were neglected."

☐ "I cannot remember *ever* being complimented for anything I did or was. I cannot *ever* remember being comforted by a touch whenever I experienced pain or illness."

☐ "I was an only child of older parents who spent far too much time focusing on 'perfecting' me. I just couldn't 'measure up.' I wasn't smart enough, pretty enough or good enough to make the grade. My parents were kind, sweet Christian people—they just chipped away at my imperfections too much and didn't praise my strengths enough."

☐ "I grew up in an alcoholic home. My dad drank. Mom was a 'rage-aholic.' She would yell and go on rampages for no apparent reason. I learned the only way I could control my mom was to shut down, not talk, and she would let me alone. Unfortunately, I used this solution on every problem I faced as I grew up."

☐ "Because I was reluctant to express myself at home for fear of being yelled at, I think I grew up to believe I didn't have much worth saying. To this day, I feel shy and my voice often shakes when I am sharing in a group."

☐ "I hate conflict. There was a large amount growing up; we were not 'permitted' to argue with my dad, and conflict would provoke severe anxiety in my mother. I have made it almost a life's work to avoid conflict as a result."

☐ "I was raised in a 'holiness' church and my family adhered to its rigid doctrines. We heard a great deal about a God of punishment and judgment and very little about a God of love. Expectations were high for a 'sinless' life which could be obtained, theoretically, as a result of 'sanctification.' Of course, this was not possible and my belief in that doctrine resulted in continual feelings of inadequacy."

As these responses indicate, the shyness which results from an unaffirming family background can be painfully debilitating.

This was also brought home to me by Dietrich, a German man in his mid-twenties whom I counseled. He held a responsible position with a major German oil firm whose managers had such respect for him that they placed him on a two-year assignment in America. He enjoyed his term here, and he told me that he didn't want to return home for fear his work would no longer be stimulating. He wanted to make a change but didn't feel there were any creative options.

I asked him what he would like to be doing by age thirty-five if God would grant his ultimate wish. The question hit a delicate nerve; he stammered and prefaced his answer with an elaborate apology. "The question is really quite academic," he said, "for what I most dream of myself doing is not at all an option. I would like to think of myself as married with a family. But that is completely out of the question."

Puzzled, I asked why. I wasn't aware of any obvious restrictions to his marrying. He responded that the problem was a morbid phobia about even broaching an intimate relationship with a woman. As we talked further, he shared of his childhood. His parents were highly critical of him and often told him he was inadequate as a person. He added that in many ways he agreed with their assessment. He was certain he did not deserve a romantic relationship.

Dietrich had so completely internalized the condemning attitude of his parents toward him that he had given up hope of making any effort to pursue his greatest desire—to become a husband and father. The tragedy is that he is a likeable, gifted man who could probably find such companionship, were he not so convinced it is unavailable.

It is not hard to understand how an unaffirming family can foster the sort of shyness that Dietrich experienced. Our parents are godlike figures to us during our formative years. Not only do we automatically internalize their judgments of us, but we assume others also share those viewpoints. If what we hear is that we are unlovable, worthless or a far sight short of perfect, we conclude this is how everyone else will likely see us. Naturally we fear extending ourselves socially, since rejection seems like such a major possibility.

We may also conclude that God shares our parents' assessment of us. This can lead us to believe, as Dietrich did, that we do not deserve a serious relationship or other good things life has to offer. And it leads us to fear God will never accept us either.

This is not to suggest that every person from a difficult family background becomes as shy as Dietrich, or even ends up shy at all. Other factors influence our development, and affirming experiences in school, church or elsewhere may give us the boost we need to overcome the effects of a negative family environment. But our family's attitude does play a major role in whether we become withdrawn.

2. *The overprotective family.* Others cite a different factor as influencing their shyness. For them an overprotective family is the problem. Their parents did too much for them and may have shielded them from making friends or facing hard experiences. The result is that they are timid about taking risks and fear striking up new acquaintances. Again the testimonies are interesting:

☐ "One of my parents taught at the school I attended. Due to her concern about retaliation from bratty students, I was not allowed to have school friends over to the house, I couldn't visit their homes, and I couldn't give my phone number to any friends. It caused me to develop an isolationist 'run and hide' lifestyle that greatly hindered me later."

☐ "My parents sheltered me from things and people I didn't know or wasn't comfortable with. They never encouraged me to step outside my comfort zone. They allowed me to be a silent, clingy child."

☐ "I remember that my parents seemed to encourage me to be more scholarly than athletic."

☐ "I was taught to think before I act, think before I talk, and be cautious of people 'bearing gifts.' "

☐ "I come from a dysfunctional family where 'secrets' were kept.

We were not encouraged or shown a way to relate in a normal fashion in interpersonal relationships. We were, however, encouraged to 'perform' in public—hence I felt comfortable with large groups and not sure where or how to act in one-on-one situations."

☐ "My parents were overprotective of me. Anything seen as 'unsafe' or potentially a mistake by their standards was wrong. So I became introverted at an early age. I wasn't allowed to speak up. And when I did not speak up, they would get mad. So either way contributed to it."

As the last example suggests, overprotective parents can be abusive ones as well. But this by no means is always the case. Often such parents are highly affirming to their children; they simply go overboard in shielding them from risks. The result can be that a seriously shy child emerges from a loving home. Sometimes, too, the responsible efforts of parents to provide a comfortable, stable home environment unwittingly have the effect of discouraging a child from taking risks.

Marie, a thirty-year-old librarian, comments, "Paradoxically, I believe my shyness is very much a function of having an above-average, stable family life that involved no moves, no changes of schools, and so on—and an extremely loving and supportive family. I would not consider it a 'sheltered' upbringing, but the extreme comfort and security of my home life unexpectedly and strongly contrasted to the insecurity of the 'real world' and made a difficult transition."

Marie's example underscores just how diverse the factors which incline us to be shy really are. While too much criticism in the family can foster shyness, too much propping up can do it as well.

3. *The family which models shyness.* While we are profoundly affected by our parents' attitudes toward us, we are also greatly influenced by their role modeling. Many in the survey note that their parents were shy. As a result, their parents did not teach

them by example how to make friends. Their family also lacked the social momentum which can help a child become outgoing. Again the testimonies:

☐ "My parents are very shy; they don't mix and mingle very easily."

☐ "My parents had bad self-images themselves. They could not possibly have taught me the skills of being assertive and confident."

☐ "My mother was afraid of almost everything, it seemed. We avoided going into towns because of 'the strangers' there, who surely meant us harm."

☐ "We were not socializers or partyers. We stayed at home most of the time."

☐ "My parents are both shy, and I see in my behavior the same patterns they have. Perhaps if we had been taken to parties or other social events when we were small, we would be more comfortable with strangers or in crowds."

☐ "My parents are shy and didn't know how to openly talk about things or make me feel comfortable with myself."

☐ "Mother was very shy, lacked self-confidence, was insecure. I felt I was leaving her out if I was confident with others while she was uncomfortable. This has left me with a lot of guilt."

While some shy parents are abusive or overprotective, many are affirming and do not place unreasonably tight reins on their children's lives. Still, their example of shyness in itself can influence their children to be shy. We absorb not only our parents' views of us but their self-images as well.

4. The out-of-the-mainstream family. Another major factor influencing shyness is a family's economic and social status. A family's financial standing can be a source of pride or embarrassment to a child. It can be especially humiliating if your family lacks the means to provide you with benefits that other children around you enjoy. Some in the survey trace the roots of their shyness to this problem:

☐ "I came from a farm family and went to school among suburbanites who didn't understand me. Our money went into the farm. Hand-me-down clothing and such made me feel out of place and inferior."

☐ "My self-esteem was *zero,* and it didn't help that we had very little money for clothes and hairdos."

☐ "I was embarrassed growing up that my family didn't have as much 'stuff' as other families. We almost never entertained. My mom seemed to value modesty over self-confidence and undercut most of my successes."

☐ "We moved from a middle-class neighborhood to a trailer in Florida when I was going into junior high. I was so ashamed for years. Family problems on top of that made me withdraw, and I was almost apologetic for existing."

Children can also be embarrassed by their parents' educational level, or by their family's cultural background or ethnic or racial distinction. Any factor which causes a child to feel "out of sync" with his peers can discourage him from reaching out socially. If it doesn't incite other children to tease him (and it probably will), he may still feel too much like an outsider to break the social inertia. In every case, it is not the trait in itself but *the fact of being different* which works against the child.

And it can work this way whether you are "one up" or "one down" from those around you. While the poor black child who lives and attends school in a middle-class white neighborhood may feel alienated from her peers and inclined to be shy, she may thrive socially in an inner-city environment where she is on equal standing with children around her. By the same token, the child of wealthy, educated parents may feel estranged in a setting where most of the children are from low-income homes. It is the fact that one's family is out of the mainstream which causes the problem.

5. *The unstable family.* It is well recognized that children of divorced or broken homes may withdraw and not reach out to their peers. They are so shell-shocked by their parents' breakup

that they are gun-shy about seeking new relationships. Any remote possibility of rejection is enough to cause them to sit still and not take social risks.

Frequent moves can also make it difficult for a child to gain a footing socially. But it does not always work this way: when a family is affirming and sensitive to a child's needs during a move, it may provide the opportunity for him or her to *gain* social confidence by making new friends. One forty-five-year-old woman tells me, "Moving a great deal as a child actually helped me face new situations. It was painful, but necessitated overcoming shyness." Children of military families typically handle moves better than most children, since relocating is part of their culture and their peers move often as well. Still, not a few military children react adversely to the frequent transplanting and become shy.

Other Background Factors
Even if someone's family background is healthy, stable and not out of the mainstream in any significant way, there are still a multitude of factors which can incline that person to be shy. Peer status is exceedingly important to most children, and anything that causes a child to be shunned or belittled by other children will contribute significantly to the growth of shyness. It takes very little to provoke children to tease another child or treat someone like an outcast. A funny name, an unusual physical characteristic, or being *too* anything (too short, too tall, too fat, too thin—any too-pronounced body features) will do it.

Many shy people see their shyness as rooted in some physical shortcoming. A thirty-eight-year-old man remarks, "In my teenage years I wasn't good-looking, so I always averted my eyes from every girl I saw, because I was sure they didn't like me. I felt like the ugliest alien who ever fell to earth. I never played with kids at school. I spoke very little and always tried to be the invisible man whenever I was around people, in hopes no one would tease me."

A twenty-five-year-old woman observes, "Being short for my age was a major factor in my shyness, especially in relationships with guys. To this day, because I'm short (and my face looks very young too), I think my guy friends tend to think of me as their little sister, rather than as someone they might want to take out on a date. This contributes to my timidness many times, also."

A forty-nine-year-old physicist notes that his shyness "originated in early childhood experiences of fighting and sorting out my place in the 'pecking order' at school. I feel that if I'd had about fifty pounds more muscle then, life would be very different for me now."

Others note that a disability such as diabetes, deafness or other physical abnormality made them overly self-conscious and subject to taunting from other children. A forty-nine-year-old woman traces her shyness to the social fallout which resulted from a childhood deformity: "I was born with a cleft palate which severely affected my speech. I have the memory of being ridiculed by classmates in the first grade because my speech was not always understandable. I imagine I learned then that it was less painful to remain silent than to participate verbally. Surgery corrected my palate and my speech, but my shyness has persisted."

Once a child is stigmatized in any way, it sticks. The label tends to be self-perpetuating and takes on a life of its own.

The Problem of Labels

Which brings us to another point—that shyness itself is a stigma. The fact that we continue to be shy can depend as much on our being *labeled* shy as anything. The labeling process is insidious. Once others get the impression we are shy, they treat us as though we are. This only increases our tendency to feel shy and to behave in ways which imply it.

Studies in the social sciences have shown repeatedly that once others gain an impression of us, it too often becomes a static picture which does not change. This is true even when the impression is inappropriate or no longer applies. The fact that others have this impression—whether accurate or not—invariably causes us to label ourselves. This helps explain why some people become shy even though their upbringing is otherwise healthy and normal. A single incident in childhood which gave others the impression they are shy can be enough to ignite the labeling process.

We should not underestimate, either, the power of the shy label in itself to keep us locked into a pattern of fearful behavior. A sixteen-year-old girl notes insightfully how this was true as she struggled with shyness in her junior-high years: "Many people—especially my mom—told me I was 'too quiet' and 'too shy.' Though I wanted to change, it made me even more shy and unconfident when I heard that."

Jesus himself, in spite of being God's Son, was so affected by negative labeling in Nazareth that "he could do no mighty work there" (Mk 6:5 RSV). It is the strongest statement of a limitation imposed on Jesus' ministry made anywhere in the Gospels. He found it necessary to move away from Nazareth in order to realize his potential and accomplish his mission. This is not to say that Jesus believed the negative labels those in Nazareth put on him. Still, it is striking that he who shared our humanity chose to operate within the bounds of these stigmas. It underlines the fact that labeling is a serious problem.

Simply being aware of the labeling process helps us avoid caving into others' expectations as we make the effort to break out of our shell. This is one of the many ways in which understanding the roots of our shyness can help us in getting better.

It is reassuring to know that while labeling can work against us, it can work for us as well. Anything we do to improve the way others see us will also help our social confidence. Fortunately, there are some important steps we can take, which we will look at in the pages ahead.

Chapter Three

The Benefits
of Shyness

Recently *a friend of mine appeared on a live national TV* program. The purpose was to discuss a book she has written on overcoming the trauma of an abusive childhood. Since I was scheduled to be interviewed on the same program in two weeks, I watched with great interest. Though this woman is an excellent writer, her public speaking experience has been minimal.

After opening pleasantries, the host began by asking her if it was difficult growing up in a dysfunctional home. My friend responded that it was extremely painful and that she and her siblings lived in constant fear of their father's frequent tirades. After several sentences, she stopped, reached for a convenient glass of water and took a generous gulp. She then continued her testimony. Her voice quivered as she related the details of a childhood laced with fear.

This is powerful, I thought. *In spite of the pressure of national TV, she is drawn into the emotion of what she's saying and is showing considerable empathy with those who suffer childhood abuse.*

The quivering stopped, but an emotional edge remained on her voice throughout the half-hour program. She skillfully fielded questions on her own past and on the challenges faced by others from abusive backgrounds.

When the program was over, I sat stunned. *This is one of the most effective TV interviews I've ever watched,* I thought. She did what is so difficult to do through the medium of television—she connected emotionally with the viewers. I knew I couldn't hope to match her performance.

Several days later I spoke with her and told her that the interview was, in a word, sensational. I mentioned that I was particularly impressed with how well she identified emotionally with her audience. Now it was her turn to be stunned. "I didn't *feel* sensational," she said. "What you saw was not empathy; I was scared to death." She went on to explain that she did not know until the moment she was escorted onto the set that this program, which she assumed would be an intimate taped interview, was to be conducted live in front of a large audience. She had ninety seconds to adjust to this startling reality and meet the host for the first time. Then came the engineer's countdown: "Five seconds to air time, four, three . . ." She froze and remained panicked throughout the program.

She added that she took the drink of water for a simple, pragmatic purpose—to pry her tongue loose. It had frozen to the roof of her mouth.

The irony in this case is that I am an experienced public speaker and pride myself in detecting the nervousness which veteran speakers cover up so well. In spite of this, I did not pick up how truly frightened my friend was. I did sense she was slightly nervous (who wouldn't be in those circumstances?), and she certainly was emotional. Yet I assumed the signs of emotion stemmed from her topic rather than from being panic-stricken.

Of one thing I have not the slightest question at all: she *was* effective in the interview. Indeed, it was a joy to tell her that the very display of humanity which she feared destroyed her effectiveness actually enhanced it considerably. My impression was shared by the producer, who told me that she and her staff were very pleased with my friend's performance.

Acceptance—The Beginning Step in Healing

The question of what constitutes a personal weakness is a delicate one. Characteristics which we look upon as weaknesses so often have their positive side as well. A feature that we consider a glaring weakness may even be perceived by others as a significant point of strength. As my friend's experience on TV brings out dramatically, others often see us quite differently than we see ourselves.

Many of us think of shyness as no more than a black scourge on our life. Far from seeing any benefits to our condition, we view it as a curse which keeps us from all the good things life has to offer. On my Shyness Survey I asked the question "Do you see any benefits to shyness? If so, what are they?" Almost one-third of those who took it either responded no, left the question blank or answered yes in a very provisional way ("if there are any benefits, they are outweighed by the problems"). A few were even indignant at the question. One person responded, "No, there are absolutely no benefits in being shy." Another, "Absolutely none. It makes my life miserable."

If we fail to see any benefits to being shy, we may view our condition as hopeless. Our limitations seem so imposing that we lack the incentive to make any serious effort to change. We feel as if we are at the bottom of a pit and the walls to be scaled for healing are simply too high and steep to climb.

In reality, we are not as deep in the pit as we might think. There *are* some benefits to being shy, even some quite significant ones. Understanding these can increase our motivation to overcome the more inhibiting effects of shyness, for we have a greater sense of beginning from a position of strength.

Appreciating these benefits also gives us a better handle on where change is really needed in our life—and where it is not. In a sense the title of this book is a bit of a misnomer, for shyness does not need to be *overcome* so much as it needs to be *modified*. My needs as a shy person are to learn how to better manage my fears, to gain some skills for interacting with others, and in general to develop a more optimistic manner of thinking. Yet there are positive aspects to my shy side which I do not want to let go of. The good news is that these features are probably so ingrained in my personality by now that they will not disappear as I become more assertive and comfortable with people. Instead they will mix in with my new features to give me an even greater effectiveness with people than I would have were I not shy in the first place.

One overriding benefit of shyness is that it acts as a buffer as we take steps to be more assertive and outgoing with people. A major reason we fear becoming more outspoken and socially active is our worry that others may perceive us as aggressive or brazen. At this point, though, we who are shy can take a deep breath and relax. Our years of being shy have built into us internal constraints which will keep us from pushing too hard. Even when we are making a determined effort to be more assertive, these subconscious checks work to our benefit, keeping us from coming across to others as arrogant or self-seeking.

Indeed, when shyness traits mix with social and assertiveness skills which we can learn, the result is often a dynamic personality which others find attractive. Assume that this will be the case as you take steps to come out of your shell. Enjoy the marvelous buffer which shyness provides!

With that thought in mind, let's look at some other benefits of the shy temperament.

☐ *Others perceive you as sincere.* Whatever the deficits of shyness, one unquestioned benefit is that shy traits contribute to the impression that you can be trusted. Others are likely to believe you are being honest and sincere in what you say.

I remember once receiving a phone call from a young man soliciting magazine subscriptions. I normally terminate such a call as swiftly as possible. (My father has a technique that works well for him. When a telephone solicitor inquires, "How are you this evening, Mr. Smith?" he instantly replies, "Terrible. Not well at all." That usually takes the caller so off guard that it is easy to end the call quickly. I don't usually go to that extreme. But I do make a point of telling the caller I am not interested in continuing the call.)

But in this case I let the man continue his pitch. The reason? He stuttered. While he knew his material well, he had difficulty getting his words out. Though I didn't know him or have any real way of reading his motives, my initial impression was that he was genuine. He did not come across like a radio announcer or a slick salesman. For this reason I felt comfortable staying in the conversation with him for a few minutes and hearing his proposal.

We who are shy often worry incessantly that others will notice any physical signals of shyness we display. Whether it is stuttering, blushing, quivering lips or hands, or a shaky voice, we dread the thought that someone will take notice of this trait and judge that we are bashful or frightened. These traits can just as well imply to another that we are believable, even that we are someone of depth. And as my friend's experience on television reminds us, others may not even detect the degree of our fear at all. They may read the physical signs as simply suggesting we feel strong emotions about the topic at hand.

As we become more assertive, we should not be concerned if physical traits or other indications of shyness do not completely disappear. They bring an important sense of balance and believability to the more outspoken personality.

☐ *Others relate to your humanness.* A related point is that others identify with our human characteristics and feel a bond with us because of them. Those with whom we interact often feel just as insecure as we do and are relieved to see indications that we have our "human side." We should not assume that others will be repelled if they sense we are shy. They are just as likely to be drawn to us.

Remember, too, that others see you not in terms of one particular characteristic (stuttering, trembling lips or such) but as a total combination of features. Traits of shyness which might not seem appealing by themselves become attractive when combined with a friendly manner and a more confident approach to people. This is a critical point to keep in mind as we seek to be more outgoing.

One of the most charming and popular individuals I know is a man who blushes frequently in public situations. Though quite shy as a youngster, he gradually learned social skills and became an effective communicator with individuals and groups. Yet the blushing brings a balance to his demeanor which, far from alienating others, endears them to him. Again, it is our humanity to which people relate. We should not be afraid of showing it.

☐ *You develop the ability to listen.* While the fears which accompany shyness can interfere with our ability to pay attention to what someone is saying, we who are shy usually learn to be good listeners for a simple reason: we are comfortable being quiet. At least fifty percent of effective listening is the ability to stay patiently silent while the other person speaks. The more assertive individual is often unable to resist the temptation to break into the conversation before the other has a fair opportunity to share his thoughts. Because the shy person is more at home being quiet, he or she more naturally develops good listening skills.

We who are shy often have a more highly developed inner life than other people, and this too contributes to our ability to listen. Our analytical nature enables us to interact internally with what someone is saying, to feel their feelings, to assess it all and give them constructive feedback.

Our ability to listen contributes to our ability to make friends. This doesn't mean we have no room for improvement. Most of us can benefit from working on our listening skills and on our ability to communicate to others that we are interested in what they have to say. But our quiet nature gives us a good starting point in this effort. It inclines us by nature to be a good listener and implies to others that we are as well.

"My dear fellow Christians, you should know this. Everyone should be quick to listen, slow to talk, slow to get angry" (Jas 1:19 Beck).

☐ *Shyness offers protection from bad company.* We don't have to look beyond Scripture to find numerous examples of friendships and relationships which were not healthy. The majority of couples described in the Bible are not pictured in a positive light. Ahab and Jezebel, Samson and Delilah, Ananias and Sapphira and many others are far from redemptive examples. Many of the friendships shown in Scripture, also, did more to pull the two individuals away from a vital relationship with God than to encourage spiritual growth. Thus we're told that after Pilate sent Jesus to Herod for interrogation, "Herod and Pilate became friends with each other that very day" (Lk 23:12 RSV). Their friendship simply served to salve their consciences over their unjust treatment of Christ and probably contributed to their moral decline rather than their mutual upbuilding.

While our shyness may keep us from good relationships, it protects us from bad ones as well. The more gregarious person is always at risk of being drawn into unhealthy associations with people. Over the years, our shyness has fine-tuned our instinctive judgment of the quality of relationships. As we begin to develop greater confidence and skill with people, this instinct helps to hold us back from those encounters which would not be good for us. Our shyness is an observation post that enables us to survey the options before committing ourselves.

☐ *You develop the ability to focus.* Though we might wish it were otherwise, none of us can realize our creative or professional potential in any area without some sacrifice of social life. If I am to develop a skill or creative interest, pursue an education or perform any job efficiently, I will need to limit my socializing in order to concentrate on the task at hand. If I am unable to tell my friends that I cannot get together with them the night before a college exam, I'll pay the price on the test the next day. Likewise, my employer will not be impressed if I take too long a lunch with friends or come to work fatigued due to partying the night before.

Part of becoming a responsible adult is learning to put appropriate restraints on our social life. The thought that we can "have it all" is a myth. There is always some trade-off involved in realizing our potential and doing our work conscientiously. As a shy person, I am able to make this trade-off more easily and naturally than the more gregarious individual. I find it more possible to focus on the aspects of work which can be done only at the expense of time with people. This ability to focus can work to my advantage as I seek to develop my talents, grow intellectually and spiritually, and do a good job for those who employ me. Ironically, the growth which takes place in my life makes me a more interesting person and broadens my social opportunities.

☐ *There are spiritual benefits.* Our shy temperament may also incline us to a deeper spiritual life and a more vibrant relationship with Christ than we might enjoy if we were not shy. This is not to say that the assertive person cannot enjoy an equally rich spiritual life. But our shyness does make us more naturally open to reaping some important spiritual benefits.

Of course, it is our shyness which drove many of us to Christ in the first place. In this case we should think of our shyness as anything but a curse, for it has opened us to the experience of Christ's abundant life. A further irony is that our fears of people have spurred us to seek a relationship with One who is able to calm our fears and give us effectiveness with people. For some of us the improvement in our ability to relate to people which has resulted from our relationship with Jesus has been remarkable.

But our shy temperament itself also works to our advantage in certain ways as we walk with Christ. Here again our ability to be quiet positions us to receive certain benefits which only come to those who take the time to be still before the Lord. There is a kind of spiritual growth and insight which can result only from periods of quiet interaction with God. Our shyness is no guarantee we will spend such time. But it does increase the likelihood that we will have the time available to invest in this way and that we will be receptive to the benefits which come from it.

The benefits which result from such private time with Christ include guidance, faith and prayerfulness.

Guidance. There is much about God's will for our lives which simply cannot be understood apart from times of quiet reflection where God has the opportunity to get our ear. While we may not hear the audible voice of God during such times, we still give him the opportunity to guide our thought process and bring us to a point of conviction about what he wants us to do. I once heard Gordon MacDonald make this point in a powerful way during a sermon on John the Baptist. He noted that John had a lot going against him; his social mannerisms were bizarre, for instance. Yet he spent great periods of time quietly before the Lord. This points out, MacDonald said, that God does not need a member of Congress, dignitary or corporation president to do his work. He will use anyone who is merely willing to take the time to listen.

We who are shy are often more willing and eager to take this time than the more assertive individual. Over time it can result in a more confident grasp of God's direction for our life.

Faith. As insight into God's will springs from times of quiet reflection before the Lord, so does faith—faith which sometimes eludes those who are busiest doing the Lord's work. From this faith comes strength to respond in obedience to what God wants us to do. The result is that the shy person sometimes surprises everyone by rising to an occasion from which others recoil.

When the soldiers came to take Jesus away for trial, none of his active followers supported him. His twelve closest companions "deserted him and fled" (Mk 14:50). During his trial and crucifixion, none of them stood by him in a meaningful way. But after his crucifixion, two unknown disciples approached Pilate and asked for permission to bury Jesus (Jn 19:38-42). John describes them both as men who had kept their distance from Jesus during his public ministry because they feared the reaction of the Jewish authorities. He notes that Joseph of Arimathea "was a disciple of Jesus, but secretly because he feared the Jews" (v. 38). Nicodemus is described as one who had "visited Jesus at night" (v. 39); while this respected Pharisee had sought Jesus out for a significant meeting (Jn 3:1-21), he did so at night to avoid detection by his comrades.

Joseph and Nicodemus were both timid men and very possibly shy. Yet when the moment of need arose, they found the strength to do something which the other disciples were afraid to do—provide Jesus with a proper burial. This is not a matter which the others would have simply overlooked, for the Jews adamantly held that the dead must be given a fitting interment. It is not hard to understand why Jesus' followers were frightened to do this, for it would mean publicly identifying with him at a time when animosity against him was at its height. But in this case two timid and unlikely men decided to throw caution to the wind. They came forth to show respect for Jesus at a time when no one else was willing to do so. In the end the weak proved strong, the strong weak.

It seems that a seed of faith had taken root in the heart of each of these men and was growing without anyone's notice. A gestation process was taking place and they were gradually gathering strength. Jesus' public disciples, on the other hand, in spite of much impressive activity with him, had not yet learned the secret of developing their inner life (Mt 26:40, 43). While they imagined they were strong (Mt 26:33-35), they were still in some ways building on a foundation of sand.

Thus it is that the shy person sometimes finds a reserve of strength to face up to a crisis where others lose heart. This will be true for each of us who takes advantage of our quiet nature to nurture an inner walk with Christ.

It is also of interest that the individual in Scripture most clearly pictured as shy—Moses—is also one of the most courageous and effective leaders in biblical history. The fears which Moses displayed when first called to deliver Egypt (Ex 3—4) and the depiction of him in the midst of his mission as "meek" (Num 12:3 RSV) indicate a man with a deep-seated shy temperament. Yet he commanded allegiance from the massive Israelite nation during its most tumultuous and challenging period—the transition time of uprooting from Egypt and moving toward Canaan. The Scriptures also describe him as one who gave close attention to his personal walk with God. In spite of the extreme demands upon him, he set aside generous time to retreat to a mountain or secluded setting to pray, meditate and interact with God. This private time with God was clearly what energized Moses for his herculean tasks. Here his shy temperament served him well, for it made him *want* to spend this time. It was not a sacrifice but a luxury to him. "The LORD would speak to Moses face to face, as a man speaks with his friend" (Ex 33:11). "Since then, no prophet has risen in Israel like Moses, whom the LORD knew face to face" (Deut 34:10).

We can take encouragement, too, from individuals in the Gospels whom Jesus commended for their faith. It is striking that, while Jesus spoke often about faith, he directly complimented someone's faith on only eight occasions. Four of these involved individuals who were healed by Jesus of a long-term ailment. They include blind Bartimaeus (Mk 10:46-52; Lk 18:35-43), the woman with the hemorrhage (Mt 9:20-22; Mk 5:24-34; Lk 8:42-48), the one leper among ten healed who thanks Jesus (Lk 17:11-19) and two blind men who ask for healing (Mt 9:27-29). While we don't know whether any of them were shy, the fact that sick people were shunned by society in New Testament times tells us that each of them would have spent considerable time alone. This seclusion apparently had its positive side, for it allowed time for the seed of faith to grow, faith which in time caught the attention of Jesus.

We who are shy should cherish the fact that we can handle solitude better than more socially active people usually can. This private time provides fertile ground which is needed for faith to blossom.

The chance to petition God. Another major benefit of private time with Christ is the chance to make specific requests of him. Scripture teaches that God waits to perform certain actions until he sees that someone is convinced enough of his power to *ask* him to act. John Calvin went as far as to say "we see that to us nothing is promised to be expected from the Lord, which we are not also bidden to ask of him in prayers."[1]

As we will note in chapter seven, there is a close connection in Scripture between gaining courage and praying for it. Yet it takes time to make requests of God, particularly meaningful requests which he is likely to take seriously. Here again the shy person enjoys a special advantage, for he or she is usually more naturally disposed to make the time for this effort.

A Possible Challenge—Shy with God

This is not to overlook the fact that shyness can infect even our relationship with God in a negative way. For a small number of shy individuals, the fears and inhibitions which they have with people are also felt when they attempt to approach God and keep them from the sort of intimacy with him they desire. On my

Shyness Survey I asked participants to indicate if their shyness hinders their relationship with Christ in any significant way. Only eight percent responded that this is the case. Most stated that their walk with Christ has helped them break the bonds of shyness in important ways. One woman noted that seeking intimacy with God was "the one place I was not shy. I knew God loved me and I could talk to him about anything."

If you do experience shyness in your relationship with Christ, it may result simply from lack of experience in a spiritual walk. You may be assuming, too, that God can only be addressed formally or with impressive language. Consider, though, the example of Moses, who spoke to God as one speaks to a friend (Ex 33:11). Remember, too, that Jesus told his disciples that he regarded them not as servants but friends (Jn 15:15), a designation he certainly meant to apply to his future followers as well. The radical news of Scripture is that God wishes to have a friendship with us—one where he prefers us to be candid and honest rather than timid or falsely pious. This becomes especially evident in the Psalms, where individuals are often brutally honest in expressing their thoughts and feelings to the Lord. Perhaps this was in the mind of the writer of Hebrews when he declared, "Let us then approach the throne of grace with confidence, so that we may receive mercy and find grace to help us in our time of need" (Heb 4:16).

If you feel shy or awkward in your relationship with Christ, let me suggest striving for a *conversational* relationship with him. Whenever you think to do it, talk to him as you would to a good friend. And set aside a few minutes each day specifically to interact with him. For now, forgo any formality or routine during that time. Put the emphasis simply on sharing your heart with Christ and reflecting on what he may be leading you to do. Tell him your concerns, ask him for healing of your shyness, and thank him for as many blessings in your life—small and great— which come to your mind. Don't worry about how polished your language is or about how "effective" your prayers may be. Simply converse with him as you would with a good companion.

However awkward you may feel in doing this, it will probably be easier to build a conversational relationship with Christ than to face the social situations you fear. And you will benefit greatly from the empowering which comes through a growing relationship with Christ. Don't shy away from this best of opportunities to confront your fears of people.

Shy Ain't Bad!

We should remember, too, the strong emphasis in Scripture upon individual uniqueness and upon each person's personality being a gift of God (Ps 139:13-16). Sometimes the tendencies that we call "shy" are actually part of the temperament God has placed within us. As we have noted, it can be part of our natural personality mix to be introverted or analytical; these are positive features which give us a vital indication of God's direction for our life. In every case the challenge is not to change our personality but to overcome the inhibitions which accompany shyness and to be certain these do not hold us back from God's best.

As we turn to consider how to combat the unhealthy effects of shyness, let me suggest one further benefit of shyness as an inspiration to spur us on. It is the fact that *our shyness puts us in position for some extraordinary experiences of adventure.* As Paul Tournier points out in his classic *The Adventure of Living,* God has put an instinct for adventure deep within each of us.[2] Our fulfillment and fruitfulness as humans mean learning to incorporate an element of adventure into our lives. Certainly when Jesus promised he would give us abundant life (Jn 10:10), this is much of what he was speaking about. He did not mean a life free of pain or challenge, but he did mean one lived on the cutting edge of adventure when we are responding in faith to his will.

The tragedy for so many people is that life becomes predictable and monotonous and the chance for adventure is smothered by the relentless routines of daily living. For a shy person, though, the very steps which others find commonplace are wrought with the potential for adventure. Discovering how to manage our fears, learning how to carry on a conversation or be assertive, gaining the courage to ask someone for a date or to speak to a crowd—as basic as these steps might be to others, they are *major* ones for us. With all of the challenge involved in taking them, there is also great opportunity for experiencing a sense of purpose as we make the effort. And even small accomplishments give us something major to celebrate. There is, in short, a substantial sense of adventure involved in the whole process of breaking the inertia of shyness.

One of our greatest needs as shy people is to become more conscious of this instinct for adventure and to learn to respond more naturally to it. It is in the midst of adventure that we feel most fully alive, and that sensation does wonders to annul our fears. Ask God to give you a deeper longing for adventure as you consider the steps in the chapters ahead. Think of these steps as a supreme—even unprecedented—opportunity for adventure. And open yourself more completely to the experience of Christ's abundant life.

Chapter Four

The Drawback of Shyness— Catastrophizing

While there are important benefits to shyness, there is a major drawback as well. The shy person worries excessively about contingencies which seldom occur. For chronically shy individuals, the problem is so serious it is fair to say they "catastrophize." They dwell on worst-case scenarios, and their predictions of disaster paralyze them from doing what they want to do. This obsessing also makes life miserable for many shy people; they feel constantly defeated by their patterns of fearful thinking.

The trepidation I felt as a teenager about asking a young woman out was a case of such catastrophizing. I worried for months about her reaction and my own as well. I dreaded that moment of truth—that split second in time when she would suddenly connect with the fact that I had been dreaming of getting to know her better. It would mean an abrupt loss of pride and the instant cracking of the protective shell I now enjoyed in not having declared any interest in her. The embarrassment would surely be too much to bear. And I greatly feared rejection, which I ranked as a substantial possibility. I was certain it would plunge me into the abyss of depression and leave indelible scars.

In time I discovered just how exaggerated my fears were. Sometimes the moment of truth did sting a bit. But the embarrassment was bearable and quickly passed. While rejection was never pleasant, I got through it and always found the resilience to move on. Then there were the wonderful serendipities, the moments of success when a date was accepted, the interest returned. The journey eventually led to a happy marriage, now coming on twenty years strong.

Many shy people never find the impetus to move beyond their obsessive fears. Expectations of the worst keep them stuck in place, afraid to take the steps they desperately want to take. The lack of momentum in their life only enhances their tendency to catastrophize, leaving them with too much room to dwell on the unpleasant consequences which might occur if they took determined action.

Some Fear of Failure Is Healthy

This is not to overlook the fact that some fear of the worst occurring is healthy and necessary to fruitful living. As a driver, for instance, it is critically important that I respect the possibility of having an accident and understand the dreadful consequences of negligent driving. Our newspapers carry stories every day of individuals who, through the sedating of alcohol or drugs, lost this fear and caused great injury as a result. We who drive need continual reminders that life can be lost or impaired in an instant through carelessness. Too much confidence is dangerous. An occasional fender-bender may even serve us well as a reality check.

The person who is too concerned with having an accident, though, is as dangerous to others on the highway as the intoxicated driver. His preoccupation with the perils of driving inter-feres with his ability to concentrate, and his nervousness robs him of the control he needs over his vehicle. Indeed, our over-riding attitude as a driver needs to be one of confidence if we are to perform effectively. While some fear of calamity needs to be in the back of our minds, it should not monopolize our thinking.

Driving is a good parallel to what our attitude should be in social situations. *Some* fear of rejection is healthy. It guards us against being presumptuous, heightens our sensitivity to others' needs and braces us for those occasional times when disappoint-ment does occur. Yet too much fear hinders our ability to relate to people. Without an overriding attitude of confidence, we find it difficult to shift our focus from ourselves to others, and the courage needed for building relationships escapes us.

This same principle holds for other areas where we take steps of faith. Some fear of failure is needed in any venture, for it heightens our alertness to the pitfalls in the way. But our pre-dominant attitude needs to be one of optimism if we are to tap into our best reserves of energy and creativity for the challenges ahead.

Catastrophizing occurs when we dwell on the worst possible case until it absorbs our thinking. With our worry sensors on overload, there is little vitality left for finding creative solutions and taking constructive action.

Shadow Boxing

What makes us prone to catastrophize? All of the factors we have looked at which foster shyness contribute to the problem. But even apart from these, we should not underestimate the sheer ingenuity of the human mind to conjure up imaginary problems. We can be brilliant at this. I once had an experience which left an indelible impression upon me about how this happens.

During my first year out of seminary I occupied the drafty attic bedroom of a hundred-year-old home which I shared with some other members of the Sons of Thunder, a Christian musical group I directed. This rundown house, an abandoned monastery bordering a cemetery, had been donated to our use for a dollar a year plus some TLC. It needed much more than we could ever give it. One look and you knew it had to be inhabited by something.

Early one morning I awakened and edged myself to the side of the bed. As the surroundings of the room gradually came into focus I realized I was staring at . . . *a bat*, clinging to the wall in front of me. I darted out of the room, slamming the door behind me, and ran downstairs yelling for help. Duane, the band's technician, calmly arose, got a broom (the standard bat-combat weapon) and marched upstairs as I tagged behind, mulling over recent news stores of rabid bats biting children in local parks. He boldly entered the room. Mustering some courage, I followed and flipped on the light switch.

The bat was no longer on the wall where I had spied him, so we began a careful search of the room, finding nothing. The windows were shut tightly, and there was no apparent way a bat could have escaped these confines. Duane concluded *I* was bats and went back to his room.

I sat down on the bed bewildered, wondering if I could have dreamed the whole thing. Finally I decided to try to go back to sleep. I reached over and switched off the ceiling light, then took a final glance at the spot on the wall where the bat had appeared.

To my astonishment, there it was! Or at least, there was a shadow with the precise dimensions of that unwelcome visitor I had glimpsed a few minutes before. I looked at the window where sunlight was pouring in and realized that a torn shade was casting a shadow on the wall, bearing a striking resemblance to a bat. The ceiling light had washed the shadow out when I turned it on.

Sitting on the bed that early morning in a semiconscious state,

I had stared at a simple shadow. But with the blurry vision of just waking up, I perceived something more. My mind registered a gigantic creature of prey about to make me a candidate for a painful series of rabies shots!

My encounter with the imaginary bat stands out in my mind as a telling reminder of my capacity to create imaginary problems. I'm reminded how easily I can envision problems where none exist and blow real ones out of proportion.

Of course, my talent for doing this is shared fairly universally among those of our species. We are uniquely gifted as humans at ruminating. We can dwell on some imagined future fiasco to the point that we are practically certain it will occur; our fears may even prevent us from taking a vital step forward. Yet so often our apprehensions bear no more relation to reality than the mirage I saw in my bedroom that morning.

The Tyranny of the Worst Possible Case

I think of the story of a young man who ran out of gas on a lonely country road. Seeing a farmhouse in the distance, he began walking up the half-mile drive toward it. After going only a short distance, he began to worry, *They probably won't have any gasoline.* As he got closer his fears increased. *If they do,* he thought, *they probably won't want to share it with me.* As he approached the farmhouse, his fears got out of hand. *They'll probably get angry with me for trespassing and order me off the premises,* he fretted. Exhausted, he arrived on the front step of the home. Before he could even knock, a smiling, elderly lady answered the door and began to say, "My dear boy! What can we do to help?"—but he cut her off, exclaiming, "Keep your blasted gasoline!" and rushed away.

Like the young man, we each have powerful mental generators capable of giving off images of failure, images which can stifle us when we want to take certain actions. We think:

☐ *She will never want to go out with me, so why bother phoning her?*

☐ *The teacher will never grant me an extension on my paper, so no sense asking.*

☐ *My friend will only laugh at me if I apologize; no use trying to talk the problem through.*

☐ *That firm will never grant me an interview. If they do, I'll certainly not impress them, so I'm better off not inquiring.*

Yet obsessing about the possibility of failure can cause each of us to miss opportunities which actually will open to us. The problem is particularly serious for those of us who are shy.

Grasshoppers and Giants

I don't know whether the twelve men whom Moses sent to spy out the land of Canaan in Numbers 13 were shy individuals. The fact that they were leaders of Israel's twelve tribes might suggest they were anything but. Yet Moses, himself a classic shy person, had appointed these men, and he may have chosen them more for their intelligence than for their courage. In any case, when they returned from their spying mission, a full ten of the twelve were able to see only immense problems in capturing Canaan, to the point of being paralyzed from going ahead with the task.

"We can't attack those people; they are stronger than we are." And they spread among the Israelites a bad report about the land they had explored. They said, "The land we explored devours those living in it. All the people we saw there are of great size. We saw the Nephilim there (the descendants of Anak come from the Nephilim). We seemed like grasshoppers in our own eyes, and we looked the same to them." (Num 13:31-33)

The men foresaw only disaster if Israel went into Canaan. What is striking is that God had already told them that they would be victorious. When God spoke to Moses about sending out the spies, he said, "Send men to spy out the land of Canaan, *which I give to the people of Israel*" (Num 13:2 RSV). The purpose of the spying escapade was not to determine whether they *could* be successful but to determine the how-tos—the logistics of the military mission. Yet the spies had such fertile imaginations that they magnified the obstacles to the point of convincing themselves that God could not possibly give them success.

One of the factors which most concerned the spies was the physical size of Canaanite men. They saw them as "Nephilim"— literally, *giants*. Archaeology has shown that the people of Canaan were indeed larger than the Israelites; the spies did not fantasize this perception. But they severely misunderstood the implications. They assumed that the men of Canaan would think of them as pushovers. "We seemed like grasshoppers in our own eyes, *and we looked the same to them.*" The evidence suggests just the opposite. Rahab the Canaanite harlot later summed it up:

> I know that the LORD has given this land to you and that a great fear of you has fallen on us, so that all who live in this country are melting in fear because of you. We have heard how the LORD dried up the water of the Red Sea for you when you came out of Egypt, and what you did to Sihon and Og, the two kings of the Amorites east of the Jordan, whom you completely destroyed. When we heard of it, our hearts melted and everyone's courage failed because of you, for the Lord your God is God in heaven above and on the earth below. (Josh 2:9-11)

Among the twelve spies only two—Joshua and Caleb—were able to see things from this perspective. "Do not be afraid of the people of the land," they declared, "because we will swallow them up. Their protection is gone, but the LORD is with us. Do not be afraid of them" (Num 14:9). The rest saw only doom. Through their powerful mental images they created problems which did not exist. And these problems, however imaginary, were fully effective in immobilizing them.

Blind Man's Bluff

A day does not go by in your life or mine when we do not confront very real problems—ones that Christ wants us to deal with prayerfully and seriously. But Satan will do his utmost to make us live in a world of illusion. He will, if he possibly can, get us to paint worst-possible-case scenarios and to dwell on them to the point that we believe them wholeheartedly.

We need to learn to recognize this thought pattern for what it is and to call its bluff when it occurs. Some recommendations for doing this will follow in the pages ahead. For now, here are three suggestions which can help us begin to resist the tendency to catastrophize:

☐ *Learn to outwit your catastrophizing.* If you find yourself worrying about a misfortune occurring in your life, remind yourself that the vast majority of calamities you envision never come about. Then take comfort: the fact you are worrying about this possibility means it will probably not occur. In other words, remember that your predictions of disaster are usually wrong and take encouragement from that! I personally find this particular mental twist quite helpful, and it often helps to jolt me out of my times of obsessing.

☐ *Learn to laugh at yourself.* One of our perennial problems as shy people is that we take ourselves too seriously. We take our ruminating too seriously and our predictions of doom too seriously. As we learn the art of laughing at our tendency to catastrophize, it will do much to bring the bats and giants down to size.

☐ *Learn to think of God's grace dynamically.* John 1:16 (RSV) promises that Christ gives "grace upon grace" to us as Christians. The Greek literally means grace following grace, or *fresh grace every split-second of our existence.* Our anxieties result in large part from trying to predict *how* God might provide grace to handle some future problem. We can never foresee this, though, for it is characteristic of grace that it is given at the moment needed and not before. The promise of Scripture is simply that when we need God's assistance, it will be there for us. In all likelihood what we dread will not occur. But if it does, God will give us exactly the grace required for handling that predicament. We need to dwell on this remarkable promise but not burden ourselves with trying to anticipate how God will do it.

Keep these suggestions in mind and do your best to apply them as we move on. In the next section we will look more closely at how to change ingrained habits of fearful thinking.

Part Two

Taking Control—
One Half-Step
at a Time

Chapter Five

Staring Fear Down

A *woman I know, Sarah, struggled with crippling stage* fright. The problem began when she was twelve and became tongue-tied giving an announcement at a church service. Her humiliation was so extreme that she went to any lengths after that to avoid speaking in front of a group.

In her thirties she became involved with a large Bible study for women. As the members came to know her, they perceived that she had gifts for leadership and teaching. They saw her potential more clearly than she did. Through much prodding and encouragement, they finally persuaded her to try teaching at one of their weekly meetings. Teaching involved giving a forty-minute lecture.

Though she was apprehensive as she began her talk, she was surprised to find that she quickly relaxed and was able to present her material coherently. Her presentation was very well received.

Most interesting is the observation she shared with me about the experience: "You know, I found I was putting as much energy into looking for ways to avoid public speaking as it took to finally go ahead and face the challenge."

Sarah's experience is so instructive, for it reminds us that we who are beset with chronic fear have two fundamental choices: we can allow the fear to continue to paralyze us and hold us back from God's best, or we can choose to take determined steps to confront and overcome it. The marvelous irony is that these steps almost always prove less frightening than the anticipation of them has been. We find it is actually easier to face them than to avoid them.

From this point on, our focus in this book will be upon how to overcome the unhealthy effects of shyness. Since serious shyness is at heart a phobia, or chronic irrational fear, it will be important to talk first of all about how to deal with the experience of fear itself. Understanding how to handle and manage fear is a critical first step in confronting any phobic situation.

If your shyness is not extreme but you are looking to this book more for advice on improving your social life, becoming more assertive or gaining a more optimistic outlook, please feel free to skip this section and move on to those chapters which are most helpful to you. But if your shyness is debilitating, as it is for so many Christians, then I recommend you begin with addressing the problem of fear itself. The perspectives raised in this chapter provide an important foundation for gaining the courage to be more outgoing.

The Fear of Fear

The greatest barrier for those of us who are seriously shy is our instinctive fear of fear itself. While we might imagine it is the prospect of rejection that most frightens us, our own reaction of fear is actually what we most greatly dread. We assume we will not be able to handle *the experience of being afraid*.

This fear of experiencing fear is at the heart of all phobias. The most common misconception held by phobia sufferers is that you must first reach the point of not being afraid before stepping into the situation you dread. This assumption keeps countless phobic individuals immobilized, hoping for some medication or miraculous change in perspective or magical cure that will dissolve their fear. Yet true healing never comes this way. At some point it is necessary to do the very thing that frightens us if we are ever to remove the lion's mask from the fear. Conquering shyness—or any fear—begins with accepting that fear itself cannot be fully avoided.

This does not mean we have to jump into the lion's den all at once. Taking small steps forward is usually the best advice. Yet even these steps will not likely seem comfortable at first. If we wait for the time when they seem completely natural, we will wait endlessly and will never break through the inertia of our fears. Phobia specialists Manuel D. Zane and Harry Milt note:

> Experience has shown, in thousands of cases, that little can be achieved in the control of phobias merely by discussing the situation in an office. There is no way a phobic person can gain control over his phobia merely by discussing it. Discussion may be a necessary prelude, a useful preparatory step. But in order to achieve actual control of the phobia, the patient has to move into the phobic situation, confront the phobic reaction, and deal with it one step at a time according to a planned strategy. We believe there is no substitute for this approach.[1]

Zane and Milt also note that those who come to them for help are usually surprised to find that experiencing fear is a vital part of the process of conquering it. While they work with many who completely overcome their apprehensions, the healing regimen always requires them gradually to confront the phobic situation.

It is no different for those of us who are shy. Healing can come only if we first learn to be reconciled to the need for experiencing some fear in the process.

Spiritualizing Fear
The point is especially critical for us to grasp as believers, for

many Christians believe it is unspiritual ever to be afraid—or even that fear itself is sin. They assume the peace of God eradicates all fear. Thus it is against God's will to take a step where fear is present.

In reality, Scripture never equates fear with sin. While it teaches that the emotion of fear may tempt us to sin, fear itself is never denoted as sinful. And while Scripture has much to say about the peace which God provides, it never promises that this peace will come *in advance* of an action we're frightened to take. Nor does it suggest that God's peace will necessarily remove all fear even when we take action.

To the contrary, Scripture is full of examples of individuals who took steps of faith even when fear was present, and never is anyone presented as out of God's will for doing so. In many cases God eased people gradually into a fearful situation rather than immersing them in it all at once. Thus Moses, terrified of public speaking, was allowed to let his brother Aaron be his spokesman when he began his mission. Still, Moses felt plenty of fear as he took the first steps into his new position; God did not overrule his psyche. While in time he gained much greater confidence, it came only through doing what he feared. Through experience he found that God both blessed his efforts and enabled him to stand firm.

There are instances in Scripture, too, where God imparted courage *before* a person was called to do something fearful. God clearly works on this level also in healing fear, a point we'll look at closely in chapter seven. Yet Scripture gives us no reason to expect that God will rid us of the need for hands-on experience in learning to handle fear. Instead, it shows that he has constructed us to need this experience as part of the healing process. There are benefits which cannot come any other way.

The Limits of Fear
One of the greatest benefits is that we discover fear is not nearly

the monster we imagined it to be. The moment of fear is seldom as traumatizing as the anticipation of it. This is a greatly liberating point to understand.

We who are shy imagine that if we step into social situations we dread, we'll be overwhelmed by fear and not be able to function. In fact, this is extremely unlikely. Psychologists observe that when a person directly confronts a phobic situation, the experience of fear is never an endless spiral leading to paralysis or breakdown. Instead, the fear recedes after a time. And when we remove ourselves from the fearful situation, relief sets in, rather than ongoing trauma. Zane and Milt observe:

> People expect "the worst" to happen in the phobic situation, but we have never seen it happen. . . . The panic mounts to a level where it seems it simply cannot be tolerated. But it does not remain at that level for long. Then it begins to recede. It may rise again briefly, but then it will also fall once more.
>
> In the vast majority of cases, people do not remain long enough in the phobic situation to find out that this is what happens. They flee when the panic attack is at its peak and, having gotten away, are convinced that they have barely escaped from a catastrophic experience from which there would have been "no return."[2]

Fear, in short, has its limits. I have often experienced the reality of this in public-speaking situations. On many occasions I've experienced stage fright when giving a talk or leading a seminar. It usually comes on during the first several minutes of facing an audience, as the realization washes over me that a large number of people are focusing their attention on *me*. The flush of fear is sometimes aggravated by the frightening thought, *What if this horrible feeling continues for the whole talk and immobilizes me? What if my panic never goes away?* Having gone through this disquieting experience on hundreds of occasions, I can happily report that the worst has never come close to occurring. In every instance the fear has passed, and usually quickly so.

The fact that fear has its limits even when we directly confront the circumstance we dread is comforting to know, for it suggests that fear will be even less tyrannical when we merely approach that situation one step at a time. As we take strategic steps to overcome shyness, we can relax in knowing that any fear we do experience will be manageable. It will not overwhelm us.

And it will pass!

Repressers and Expressers

Here is another encouragement. People with phobias fall into two categories: those who repress their fear and those who don't. The fearful flyer who represses the fear, for instance, does not think about being frightened to fly before getting on the plane. This person keeps busy packing for the trip, rushing to the airport and going through the logistics of ticketing and boarding. Only once the cabin doors slam shut does panic set in. The fear is particularly unsettling because it has not been anticipated.

The phobic flyer who does not repress feelings, on the other hand, feels the fear profoundly before the trip but is often surprised to find the anxiety level much less than anticipated once the plane is aloft. I understand this phenomenon well, being the white-knuckled sort who does not repress. If I do feel frightened during the flight, I'm not startled by the feeling for I fully expected it. This anticipation takes a significant edge off the fear. To my pleasant surprise, I am usually not terribly anxious once the plane is airborne (though I do start worrying about my next trip).

We who are shy are usually not repressers. Far from it! We dwell on the horrible things we imagine might happen if we became more outgoing. There may not seem to be much advantage to this obsessing; indeed, it works against us in many ways. But the fact that we do not repress our fear is in itself psychologically healthy. Because we feel our fear so strongly *before* we enter certain social situations, we will not likely experience the same magnitude of fear in the situation itself. This is the remarkable paradox of not repressing.

Again, Milt and Zane document the truth of this paradox in their work with phobia sufferers. "We can assure those . . . who have some concern about going into the phobic situation that what they will actually experience will not be nearly as bad as they may anticipate it to be. We have it on the testimony of hundreds of patients that, almost invariably, the anticipation is much worse than the reality."[3]

This surprising truth about fear is wonderfully reassuring as we make the effort to break out of our shell. The fact that we do not repress our fear means it will be less of a factor once we are in motion. We can also take relief in knowing that we do not have to go through the heroics of denying our fear. In reality, as we grit our teeth and clench our fists and tell ourselves repeatedly "I am not afraid," our apprehension only grows. Against such denial, Milt and Zane counsel, "When fear comes . . . let it be."[4] But we can take relief, too, in knowing that the moment of reality will not be as traumatizing as our anticipation of it has been.

You Can Handle It
You have far more capacity to experience fear and remain unscarred than you probably realize. God has put an extreme measure of resilience within each of us. He has also given us each a striking capacity to stand up under tension and even be at our best potential under a certain measure of stress.

In his book *The Joy of Stress* (yes, that is the actual title), Canadian physician Peter G. Hanson notes that a reasonable measure of stress in life not only spurs us to realize our fullest potential but also contributes to our emotional and physical health. Hanson argues that many Americans would enjoy longer life spans if they did not bail out of stress as they become more comfortable financially.[5]

His conclusions agree well with Scripture, and I believe they help to explain some of the remarkable life spans of saints in the

Old Testament. It seems clear that those who enjoyed great longevity also remained active in old age. The benefit wasn't only long life but also alert and energetic life. Thus we're told that Moses "was a hundred and twenty years old when he died, yet his eyes were not weak nor his strength gone" (Deut 34:7).

For many it is something of a revelation to discover that stress can be healthy. While not all stress is good for us, we can rest assured that the anxiety we experience in the effort to overcome a phobia is not harmful to us. It will not lead to our impairment or breakdown but will be liberating in its effects.

You may be thinking of examples which prove the opposite. What about shell-shocked soldiers? They are emotionally crippled from the trauma of war. Doesn't their example prove there is grave danger in exposing ourselves to a situation we fear? Don't we run the risk of a similar emotional breakdown?

There is a world of difference between these two situations. A soldier suffers shell shock because of repeated exposure to battle situations where his life was in unquestioned peril. The phobic situation is not genuinely life-threatening (even though it feels that way to us). Our fear greatly outstrips the actual risk involved. When we actually do confront what we dread, we discover there is much less to fear than we supposed. And as we grow accustomed to the fearful situation, our anxieties diminish.

There is simply no evidence in psychological studies that systematically confronting a phobic situation ever leads to the sort of emotional breakdown suffered by shell-shocked soldiers. Instead, emotional liberation always results from the effort. This is remarkably good news for those of us who are shy.

But now for some further good news. Not only is our capacity to handle fear probably more ingrained than we realize; there are also practical steps we can take to substantially reduce the impact of fear in any situation. We will look at these closely in the next chapter.

Chapter Six

Breaking the
Panic Cycle

A *friend of mine loved to quote Daniel 5:6 from the King* James Version. The verse describes King Belshazzar's horror when a hand appeared from nowhere and inscribed a mysterious message on the palace wall. "Then the king's countenance was changed, and his thoughts troubled him, so that the joints of his loins were loosed, and his knees smote one against the other."

I confess my friend quoted this verse not for inspiration but for comic relief. The archaic language amused him, especially the reference to joints loosening and knees smiting.

Apart from his humorous intentions, there is actually a serious point which this verse calls to our attention. It's the fact that fear always produces a physical reaction. In the case of intense fear, the physical symptoms are particularly obvious.

This point is taken for granted by the authors of Scripture. Consider, for instance, how often the Bible couples fear with the physical response of trembling. "Fear and trembling" are men-

tioned together in a single phrase throughout Scripture. Biblical
writers simply assumed that acute fear will be accompanied by a
physical reaction of some sort.

We who suffer from phobic fear need little convincing this is
true. Whether it is the fear of bridges, the dread of elevators or
the apprehensions associated with shyness, the fact remains the
same: We feel our fear physically as well as emotionally.
Trembling is usually involved. Our stomach may knot up, our
knees weaken, our muscles tighten, our back feel out of joint.
We also perspire more readily and without fail our heart beats
faster and our breathing accelerates.

We understand this phenomenon well, and being reminded
of it is not particularly uplifting. There is a fascinating corollary
to this, though, which is seldom well understood. While fear
triggers physical reactions, it is just as true that controlling these
reactions reduces fear. To stop the knocking knees is to quell
the feeling of fear as well.

There are several reasons it works this way. For one thing, our
emotional and physical responses are closely connected. Because fear produces certain physical responses, we learn from
the earliest age to associate these symptoms with the feeling of
fear. When these symptoms occur, they increase our fear, which
in turn provokes the symptoms.

Let's say, for instance, that fear causes the muscles in my arms
to tighten. That taut feeling reminds me that I'm afraid, and so
perpetuates my sense of panic. The feeling of fear, of course,
sustains the tension in my arm muscles and a panic cycle ensues.
Any step, though, which reduces the stiffness in my arms also
reduces my feeling of panic, for the physical cue is gone. The
cycle of fear has been broken.

In addition, physical relaxation in general leads to emotional
relaxation and thus reduces fear. Any step which increases our
general well-being has a sedating effect upon fear, and physical
relaxation contributes significantly to our well-being.

Then there is the fact of personal control. A major reason we panic is that we sense we are losing control. Most frightening is the thought that we have no control over our emotions, that we are slipping into the abyss, so to speak. Any step which restores our sense of personal control also reduces our feeling of fear. Simply discovering we can alter our physical response to fear does wonders to increase our sense of control and thus to alleviate our fear.

Reversing the Effect

With these thoughts in mind, here are several suggestions for countering your physical reactions to fear:

☐ *Practice abdominal breathing.* When we're stressed, our need for oxygen increases. Typically we breathe more intensively but into our chests. This shallow "thoracic" breathing results in part from our esteem for the military posture—"stomach in, chest out!" Yet in this position our lungs are not able to expand to receive their full capacity of air. The result is that we feel the need to breathe more quickly, and hyperventilation may occur. When under stress, we need to counter our natural tendency toward chest breathing. Let your stomach relax (and hang out if necessary!), then inhale slowly and deeply into it. Hold your breath for several seconds, then slowly let it out. The tranquilizing effect is remarkable. Continue doing this until your sense of control returns.

☐ *Relax muscles you tend to tense.* The next time you feel panic coming on, make a point of noticing your muscular responses. Do you clench your hands? Cross your legs tightly? Fold your arms? Tighten your stomach muscles? Push your toes together? Many of us who, like myself, have a frontal bite, clench our teeth. All of these reactions increase our stress levels. The clenched jaw, in fact, can produce a number of other unfortunate side effects, including dizziness, distortion in the ear, migraines and facial pain.

Learn to identify your muscular reactions under stress, then make a conscious attempt to counter your natural inclinations. Practice relaxing your muscles when you feel tense. Open your hands and let them hang loosely. Let your jaw hang limp. Resist the temptation to cross your legs or clamp them together. Move your head from one side down onto your chest and then over to the other side, then back, to loosen your neck. When relaxing the muscles is combined with proper breathing, the physical effects of stress and panic are greatly reduced. As a phobic flyer I can attest that these simple techniques have done wonders for reducing my uneasiness when airborne. They have helped reduce my anxiety in public-speaking situations as well. All of us can experience a greater measure of control over our anxiety responses when these practices are followed.

☐ *Follow a healthy routine of rest, eating and exercise, and management of your time.* In general, anything which contributes to our physical well-being helps to reduce our overall stress level. Giving your body proper sleep (with the help of a warm bath or whatever helps you most), taking time for a morning walk instead of jumping into the stress again as soon as you wake up, having a vigorous game of handball or tennis—these ways of taking care of yourself are great antistressors.

Like many people, my appetite diminishes when I'm anxious or fearful. I find, though, that when I neglect my normal eating habits, my vulnerability to being anxious increases. If I'm feeling nervous about a talk or a trip, I think of eating as an act of discipline at that time (at other times it's a wonderful celebration, but not now). I go ahead and eat a normal meal, even though I'm not particularly eager to do so. Again and again I find the simple step of keeping food in my stomach reduces stress. If you tend to find comfort in lots of junk food at stressful times, limiting yourself to nutritious meals and snacks can save you from the overfull feeling and the "sugar high" which go along with that.

BREAKING THE PANIC CYCLE

And because so often we're behind on obligations, so that our time seems out of control along with everything else, we can reduce stress through finding time management techniques. Perhaps carrying the pile of paperwork from your desk to the room where the TV is will allow you to sort while you watch, and lots of the clutter can be eliminated. Then when you do get an hour at your desk, it won't be so scary and you can concentrate on handling the most important pieces of paper. The usual horrible-desk sense of defeat will be replaced by a sense of accomplishment.

An Appropriate Concern

I once gave suggestions for managing the physical effects of fear when speaking at a large college retreat. The remarks took no more than ten minutes and were a small portion of my five hours of lecturing that weekend. A week or so later I received a detailed typewritten letter from a staff person calling me to task for encouraging Christian students to practice—*yoga!* Remembering his concern reminds me that there are Christians, even quite intelligent ones, who shoot up red flags as soon as you broach the subject we're considering. At best they feel the topic has no relation to spiritual life. At worst they fear you are caving in to Eastern philosophy or New Age ideas.

My purpose in recommending physical means for reducing fear is far from suggesting these might be the basis for a spiritual philosophy. I'm simply concerned that we understand our being as God has created it and learn to be the best steward of it we can. We dishonor God, in fact, if we do not take advantage of an obvious means he has provided for solving a problem. We are guilty of spiritualizing if we ignore the solutions he has built into human life and then expect him to meet our needs in a more direct way.

The Burned-Out Prophet

In fact, Scripture gives us a vivid picture of the principles we are talking about in 1 Kings 19:1-8. The prophet Elijah is burned out, at the end of his emotional and physical strength—the result of a victorious but brutally exhausting encounter with the prophets of Baal. When a messenger brings him a death threat from Queen Jezebel, he panics. Fleeing to the wilderness, he abandons his servant, then asks God to take his life. God's response? He sends an angel to provide water and bake a cake for Elijah (yes, I know, the first angel-food cake), and gives him the grace to sleep peacefully.

After several days of such rest and relaxation his energy returns. "So he got up and ate and drank. Strengthened by that food, he traveled forty days and forty nights until he reached Horeb, the mountain of God" (1 Kings 19:8). What is fascinating to observe in this incident is that God healed a person who was severely traumatized by ministering to his *physical* needs.

We can take heart that managing our physical life with an eye to reducing our vulnerability to fear not only makes sense psychologically but is fully in accord with God's will.

Other Emotions Cancel Out Fear

There's still more to be said about controlling fear, though. We can reduce the sensation of fear not only through the way we manage our physical life but through how we manage our *thought life* as well.

Psychologists observe that the human psyche is so constructed that we cannot experience the impact of two emotions at the same time. The woman who is drawn into the rapturous music of a classical concert is not feeling anxious about the financial woes which troubled her to the point of distraction only a few hours before. The emotion of joy has effectively canceled out the emotion of anxiety. This understanding leads many phobia specialists to recommend that those with chronic fear make the conscious effort to concentrate on pleasant and encouraging images. To the effect that these thoughts occupy one's attention, they take the place of fearful musings.

The phobic flyer, for instance, is encouraged to dwell on a pleasant, relaxing scene—a balmy afternoon sunbathing at the beach, or a quiet walk in the mountains—when panic over flying sets in. Such imaging helps to displace the visions of fiery air crashes that fill the panicky flyer's mind, and the peace of mind which comes from dwelling on these pleasant thoughts itself reduces the sensation of fear (affecting even our body chemistry).

A similar approach works for those of us who are shy. For us the problem is the fear of people, and this is where our catastrophizing occurs. If it seems too artificial to imagine successful future encounters with people, we at least should make the effort to dwell on successes God has given us in the past and on good memories which encourage us. We should regard this practice as exercising good stewardship over our thought process. Paul points to the importance of such mental discipline in Philippians 4:8, when he advises, "Whatever is true, whatever is noble, whatever is right, whatever is pure, whatever is lovely, whatever is admirable—if anything is excellent or praiseworthy—think about such things." He clearly teaches that we should make a conscious effort to avoid ruminating and to focus on encouraging and redemptive thoughts.

Action Triumphs over Fear

A closely related point is that *anything* we do to deal directly with the details of a situation we fear has the effect of taking our attention off our fear and thus reducing it.

This principle is a central part of the strategy followed in many phobia treatment programs. The person who is fearful of bridges, for instance, is urged to focus on details of the bridge and its surroundings. He feels the railing, stamps his feet to sense the firmness of the pavement, counts the cars coming across, observes the intricacies of the structure, examines the scenery around the bridge. This type of focused concentration not only diverts his attention from his apprehension but increases his sense of control in the phobic situation.

We who are shy will find this same approach helpful. Let's suppose you have just arrived at a party or social function and are feeling panicky. Make an effort to focus on the details of your surroundings. Feel the bounce of the carpet under you, lean against the wall, touch the velvet in a chair, observe the features of a painting; maintain as much tactical contact with the setting as you can. Then, even more important, focus on the person or persons with whom you are speaking. Give your attention as fully as possible to listening to what they say. Think about them, observe details about them, consider what emotions and inhibitions they may be feeling. This concentration on surrounding details and individuals will work greatly to your benefit in reducing anxiety.

Thought-Stopping

Finally, I want to recommend that you make a more direct frontal attack on the problem of catastrophizing. It is particularly helpful to follow the practice of "thought-stopping." This approach, advised by specialists who work with phobia sufferers, involves a determined effort to halt obsessive thinking the moment it begins.

When an unreasonable fear comes to mind, immediately yell internally (or aloud, if no one is around) *"Stop!!!"* It may help to picture a police officer holding up a large stop sign, blowing a whistle incessantly and commanding you to stop. Be absolutely consistent in doing this every time an irrational thought troubles you. Insist that it cease and desist. Then immediately replace the fearful thought with a pleasant one. Think of a situation which you find relaxing or encouraging. Remind yourself, too, of God's absolute care for you, his desire for your very best, his gracious forgiveness which is available to you personally, and his complete acceptance of your feelings.

The important thing, specialists point out, is being consistent and persistent in this response. Over time, when combined with other practices we're suggesting, thought-stopping helps considerably to change patterns of fearful thinking.

Taking Heart As You Take Control

Fear does not have to ruin your life or control it. You have much more capacity to manage and control your fear than you probably thought. But if you are shy, chances are good fear often gets the better of you. You probably spend more energy than you would like to admit looking for ways to avoid social situations you fear.

I urge you to take this same energy and invest it in confronting these situations. You will almost certainly find that moving forward is less frightening than standing still. I promise you, too, that if you follow the suggestions in this section, you will be able to handle challenges far greater than you think. With time and effort you will see a significant improvement in your confidence level with people. And fear itself will become much less of a hindrance in what you choose to do.

Indeed, this is one of those intriguing points in the Christian life where your greatest weakness can become your greatest strength.

Chapter Seven

Praying for Courage

Many Christians tell me that their relationship with Christ has been a major factor in overcoming shyness. They speak of the courage which has come through that relationship and how it enables them to relate to people more confidently.

Of course, the skeptic may wonder whether authentic spiritual change has really taken place in such cases or whether it has merely been the power of suggestion at work. If someone believes Christ has healed certain fears, for instance, isn't it possible that the *belief* is what causes the fear to diminish?

Undoubtedly, the power of suggestion does play a role at times. Yet I have seen many cases where I'm convinced something far more significant than the power of suggestion is involved. One such example is Maureen. She claims that victory over shyness has come through God's direct intervention in her life, resulting from her experiences in prayer and worship. "I've been helped a lot in the past few years by my ability to abandon myself to worship," she says. "When I became able to do this, I would stop (at least for periods of time) being controlled by what others might think. I was even able to be worship leader at my small church, for a time. I feel a greater excitement in my relationship with the Lord than I ever have."

What convinces me that Maureen has experienced a genuine spiritual transformation is the fact that she was fifty years old when this healing began to take place. She had been chronically shy throughout her life until that time. Roots of shyness which run this deep do not respond well to mere efforts of positive thinking or the power of suggestion alone. I believe she has experienced God's direct healing touch in a significant way.

The testimony of numerous Christians to this sort of experience, the pervasive testimony of Scripture to the transforming power of God, and my own experience all lead me to a deep-seated conviction that God does work directly in our lives to impart courage and the healing of fear. The danger of stressing this too early in a discussion of shyness is that we may be dissuaded from doing what we can personally to overcome our fears. *All* healing ultimately comes from God. Yet God uses a variety of means to bring about healing, including our own effort, the action of others, and his direct intervention. Obedience requires that I be open to God's bringing healing through human means as well as directly.

If I suffer from cancer, for instance, I am spiritualizing if I merely sit still and expect God to heal me without taking advantage of medical options available. God often uses human channels in healing, and I open myself to his help most fully by availing myself of the best medical assistance I can find. But God also heals cancer directly, apart from any human effort. In many cases we find that he uses both human and direct means to heal, and both have their purpose. Through taking initiative to seek medical help, I grow in learning responsibility and stewardship for my life; through experiencing God's direct healing, I find my faith is strengthened and my dependence upon Christ is deepened.

These same dynamics prove true in emotional healing, including healing of the fears which accompany shyness. I should do everything possible from the human angle to overcome my fears and increase my confidence with people. I should follow practical steps for breaking the grip of fear and for improving my social and assertiveness skills. I should make a determined effort to think more optimistically and to break with my habit of always expecting the worst. At the same time I should look earnestly and expectantly to God for help, even for a healing miracle. I should ask him to grant the fullest measure of help which he is willing to provide. I should pray for courage to face people and ability to relate to others that goes well beyond my natural skills.

Divine Comfort

I may take heart, too, in knowing that God honors requests such as these. These are not likely to be prayers which bounce off the ceiling. As is often said, "Be careful what you pray for, for you shall surely get it!"

The Bible provides abundant evidence that God is concerned with healing the fears of those who follow Christ. Time and again Scripture shows that he is sensitive to our fears and seeks to give us courage to rise above them. Consider how often this situation takes place in Scripture: Someone is confronted by God, by an angel or by Jesus himself, and is struck with terror at the divine presence. Immediately the person is told, "Do not be afraid." Usually it is clear that this mere command brings prompt relief and great strength of heart to the frightened person. It announces that the authority of the Creator of the universe is on his or her side. These four simple words assure the person that God does not intend to harm but will protect and empower for the mission ahead.

The Old Testament hero Daniel, known for being fearless, lets us in on a terrifying experience he had—a vision after which "I had no strength left, my face turned deathly pale and I was helpless" (Dan 10:8). A hand touched him. "Do not be afraid, Daniel," the angel counseled. "Since the first day that you set your mind to gain understanding and to humble yourself before your God, your words were heard, and I have come in response to them" (10:12).

Daniel continues his description of this remarkable incident: Then one who looked like a man touched my lips, and I opened my mouth and began to speak. I said to the one standing before me, "I am overcome with anguish because of the vision, my lord, and I am helpless. How can I, your servant, talk with you, my lord? My strength is gone and I can hardly breathe."

Again the one who looked like a man touched me and gave me strength. "Do not be afraid, O man highly esteemed," he said. "Peace! Be strong now; be strong."

When he spoke to me, I was strengthened and said, "Speak, my lord, since you have given me strength." (10:16-19)

As God spoke to Daniel, so he addresses us when we are troubled with unreasonable fear, telling us, "Do not be afraid." We should dwell on this thought and take great encouragement from it.

It is in this same spirit that so many passages of Scripture urge us not to be fearful:

☐ "Do not be afraid. Stand firm and you will see the deliverance the LORD will bring you today. . . . The LORD will fight for you; you need only to be still" (Ex 14:13-14).

☐ "Do not be afraid of any man, for judgment belongs to God" (Deut 1:17).

☐ "See, the LORD your God has given you the land. Go up and take possession of it as the LORD, the God of your fathers, told you. Do not be afraid; do not be discouraged" (Deut 1:21).

☐ "The LORD himself goes before you and will be with you; he will never leave you nor forsake you. Do not be afraid; do not be discouraged" (Deut 31:8).

☐ "The Lord is a stronghold for the oppressed, a stronghold in times of trouble. And those who know thy name put their trust in thee, for thou, O Lord, hast not forsaken those who seek thee" (Ps 9:9-10 RSV).

☐ "The LORD is my light and my salvation—whom shall I fear? The LORD is the stronghold of my life—of whom shall I be afraid? When evil men advance against me to devour my flesh, when my enemies and my foes attack me, they will stumble and fall. Though an army besiege me, my heart will not fear; though war break out against me, even then will I be confident" (Ps 27:1-3).

☐ "Thou didst hear my supplications, when I cried to thee for help. Love the Lord, all you his saints! . . . Be strong, and let your heart take courage, all you who wait for the Lord!" (Ps 31:22-24 RSV).

☐ "I sought the LORD, and he answered me; he delivered me from all my fears. Those who look to him are radiant; their faces are never covered with shame. This poor man called, and the LORD heard him; he saved him out of all his troubles. The angel of the LORD encamps around those who fear him, and he delivers them. Taste and see that the LORD is good; blessed is the man who takes refuge in him. Fear the LORD, you his saints, for those who fear him lack nothing" (Ps 34:4-9).

☐ "God is our refuge and strength, an ever-present help in trouble. Therefore we will not fear, though the earth give way and the mountains fall into the heart of the sea, though its waters roar and foam and the mountains quake with their surging. . . . The LORD Almighty is with us" (Ps 46:1-3, 11).

☐ "My son, keep sound wisdom and discretion; let them not escape from your sight, and they will be life for your soul and adornment for your neck. Then you will walk on your way securely and your foot will not stumble. If you sit down, you will not be afraid; when you lie down, your sleep will be sweet. Do not be afraid of sudden panic, or of the ruin of the wicked, when it comes; for the Lord will be your confidence and will keep your foot from being caught" (Prov 3:21-26 RSV).

☐ "Fear not, for I am with you, be not dismayed, for I am your God; I will strengthen you, I will help you, I will uphold you with my victorious right hand. . . . For I, the Lord your God, hold your right hand; it is I who say to you, 'Fear not, I will help you' " (Is 41:10, 13 RSV).

☐ " 'For I know the plans I have for you,' declares the LORD, 'plans to prosper you and not to harm you, plans to give you hope and a future' " (Jer 29:11).

☐ "I called on your name, O LORD, from the depths of the pit. You heard my plea: 'Do not close your ears to my cry for relief.' You came near when I called you, and you said, 'Do not fear.' O Lord, you took up my case; you redeemed my life" (Lam 3:55-58).

☐ "Let the weak say, 'I am strong!' " (Joel 3:10 KJV).

☐ "Do not let your hearts be troubled and do not be afraid" (Jn 14:27).

☐ "For God did not give us a spirit of timidity, but a spirit of power, of love and of self-discipline" (2 Tim 1:7).

☐ "Do not be anxious about anything, but in everything, by prayer and petition, with thanksgiving, present your requests to God" (Phil 4:6).

The Holy Spirit's Role

It is also greatly reassuring to realize how central the function of giving courage is to the Holy Spirit's role in our lives. It is hard to exaggerate the emphasis given to this aspect of the Holy Spirit's work in Scripture. Jesus pointed to this when he used the term *counselor* to refer to the Holy Spirit, whom he promised to send to his disciples (Jn 14:16, 26; Jn 15:26; Jn 16:7). The Greek term for "counselor" meant a military official responsible for encouraging troops who had lost their courage in the face of battle. He was a motivator, in the most profound and challenging sense. Jesus could scarcely have used a more significant figure to portray the Holy Spirit as one who imparts courage.

When we look at how Scripture pictures the influence of the

Holy Spirit in people's lives, we find it gives considerable attention to his role as a motivator. Take a concordance and trace references to the Spirit in the Old Testament, and you will see what I mean. So often when the Holy Spirit comes upon someone the effect is that a timid, insecure, ambivalent person is suddenly charged with confidence to do something he had thought was beyond himself.

Gideon's experience in Judges 6 is a good example. There are few heroes of the Bible who suffered from lower self-esteem. When the angel approached Gideon and announced that he would lead Israel to defeat the Midianites, Gideon complained, "How can I save Israel? My clan is the weakest in Manasseh, and I am the least in my family" (Judg 6:15). He feared not only the formidable Midianites but also his own people, who had degenerated to idol worship. Even though God provided him with several proofs to convince him he would be successful, Gideon could only respond to God's commands faintheartedly at first. Thus when told by God to destroy his father's Baal-idols, "Gideon took ten of his servants and did as the LORD told him. But because he was afraid of his family and the men of the town, he did it at night rather than in the daytime" (Judg 6:27).

Yet a critical change occurred when Gideon was roused by the Holy Spirit. Judges 6:34-35 explains, "Then the Spirit of the LORD came upon Gideon, and he blew a trumpet, summoning the Abiezrites to follow him. He sent messengers throughout Manasseh, calling them to arms, and also into Asher, Zebulun and Naphtali, so that they too went up to meet them." Gideon's motivation increased markedly at the moment the Holy Spirit fell on him. Though his fears did not completely disappear, he was stirred by courage that overshadowed his fear.

We find a different but no less inspiring picture of the Holy Spirit giving motivation in Exodus 35:30—36:2. Here Moses seeks workers to help construct the sanctuary in the desert. Bezalel, the first individual in Scripture described as filled with the Spirit, is pictured as deeply motivated to use his skill of craftsmanship and "inspired" to teach (Ex 35:34 RSV). Others are described as having hearts "stirred . . . up" to employ their particular gifts in the project (Ex 36:2 RSV).

If you know Christ as your Lord and Savior, then the promise of Scripture is clear: his Spirit resides in you (Rom 8:9-11). As he energized Gideon, Bezalel and so many others in Scripture, he is offering you the courage to live life wholeheartedly—to take steps he wants you to take toward building relationships, using your gifts and sharing his love with the world. There are things you must do to experience this courage, adjustments in your lifestyle and thinking. Yet rest assured that God is on your side as you seek a more courageous approach to life.

Though it is from an apocryphal text, there's a statement which beautifully reflects the same picture of Christ as a motivator that we see so consistently proclaimed in Scripture: the Gospel of Thomas has Jesus declaring, "He who is close to me is close to the fire."

An Open Channel

While the Bible speaks extensively about God giving courage, it also has much to say about our ability to access this benefit. Here again the message of Scripture is a profoundly encouraging one, for we are told emphatically that we can gain courage by praying for it. Jesus promised that God would give the Holy Spirit in rich measure to anyone who asks for it (Lk 11:13). When we consider that one of the Holy Spirit's central roles is imparting courage, the promise assures us that inner strength is available through asking—that is, through prayer.

In addition, when we look carefully at the biblical perspective on prayer, we find that the most significant function of prayer is to draw on God's strength. Through prayer I put myself in position for God to work within me, to give me the will to carry out what he wants me to do and the courage to do it.

Consider how Jesus dealt with his apprehensions in the Garden of Gethsemane. In Gethsemane we see the humanity of Jesus in fullest relief, for he actually pleads with God to take the responsibility from him. "My Father, if it is possible, may this cup be taken from me" (Mt 26:39). He goes an important step further, though, and in the same verse prays, "Yet not as I will, but as you will." He asks God to strengthen him for the purpose he knows he must accomplish. His prayer is for courage, for victory over his fears. He prays intensively in this way for a considerable period, begging for resolve to complete his mission.

Jesus comes forth from the garden with a new heart, capable of bearing up under the unfathomable emotional and physical stress of the days ahead. His disciples, who ignore his admonition to pray for strength (Mt 26:40), fall apart. Though they have expressed a strong desire to stand with him (Mt 26:33-35), they are unable to rise to the occasion when the situation becomes life-threatening.

The lesson, so obvious yet so easily overlooked in the frantic pace of modern life, is that through prayer we gain emotional strength which otherwise may elude us.

Reaping the Benefits

From the Gethsemane incident we learn that we can benefit greatly from a period of concentrated prayer asking for courage and the healing of our fears. In Gethsemane Jesus urged his disciples to spend "one hour" praying for inner strength (Mt 26:40). I do not believe he meant anything rigid by this time reference. The ancients did not have the precise time measurements we have today. The day was divided into twelve equal hours of daylight and twelve of night, and since time was measured by the sundial, hours were slightly longer in the summer than in the winter. By counseling his disciples to pray for one hour, he was telling them to give a significant period of time to praying.

Just as he himself was doing, they needed to confront their feelings thoroughly and allow time for God to comfort and strengthen them for the challenge ahead. Substantial time was needed for this sort of interaction with God.

Our own situation is no different. When we are facing a significant challenge or are held back by fear from doing what God wants us to do, we should pray earnestly that he will give us strength of heart. It is usually a good idea to set aside a specific and generous period of time to petition for his help. If shyness is a serious problem for you, I strongly recommend that you do this.

How much time should you spend praying in this way? An hour is a good benchmark. But if you can handle a longer segment—a morning, an afternoon or a whole day—there can be special benefits which come from praying for such an extended period.

Plan to spend this time in an inspiring setting where you would not expect to be interrupted. Pick a situation that works well for you; it might be a sanctuary, a park where you can sit or walk, a hotel room, a drive in the country. Think of this time as a personal retreat to pray for healing of your shyness.

As you pray, thank God for the benefits of your temperament. Ask him to help you appreciate the uniqueness of the personality he has put within you. But pray also for healing of the unhealthy fears which keep you back from his best intentions for your life. Ask him to give you resolve to follow his will and courage to relate to people at all points where this is needed. Then consider carefully specific steps you can take to lessen the control of fear in your life and to realize your potential for Christ. Be alert for his direction. Determine before him to take the steps which come to mind, and pray for the inner strength to do so. Then ask him to open doors as you move forward and to give fruit to your efforts.

As you pray, review portions of Scripture which emphasize

God's role in healing fear and giving courage. Ask him to make the truth of these passages a reality in your life. Enjoy the promises and reassurances which they bring. Write down insights, prayers or resolves, so that you won't forget what God helps you discover during your study and prayer.

I urge you to give this idea of the personal retreat a try. Most Christians whom I ask tell me they have never taken a private retreat to pray about any matter. With all of the demands upon them, it seems too difficult to make the time needed for such uninterrupted prayer. As a shy person, you are probably more accustomed to time alone. Take full advantage of your ability to handle solitude, and give some meaningful time to fervent prayer for God's healing and strengthening. Then rest assured that you are enjoying benefits of that time as you move forward.

Good Habits

I also recommend that you make a practice of praying for courage daily, during your regular devotional time. This does not have to be a major part of your quiet time; a minute or two given to asking God for strength may be adequate. But make the point of asking Christ to strengthen you for the challenges of the day ahead and to give you special grace for all of the encounters with people you will face. Pray that he will either remove your fear or give you the courage to face these situations in spite of your fear. Ask for an abiding sense of his presence and the confidence that he is upholding you in every situation you enter. Trust that the courage you pray for will be provided. Scripture shows that this is a request God is exceedingly willing to grant.

Finally, let me remind you of the considerable benefits which can come from praying and praising God together with other Christians. The Sunday worship service often provides the best opportunity for doing this. We should not take lightly the possibility that God will give us fresh courage or even special healing in this setting. This was the experience of Maureen, the woman mentioned earlier in this chapter. Though excessively shy for five decades, she found surprising help through her experiences in worship.

The bottom line is that we each should take those steps which best allow Christ to empower our lives. As we come to appreciate more fully how he is able to strengthen us, we will find it more natural to spend the time in communion with him which opens us to his help. As Christians we enjoy a benefit for combating the fears of shyness—a benefit which goes unrecognized by most people. Let us take full advantage of the power of Christ which is available to us in such extraordinary measure. This is one area where we do not want to settle for reduced benefits.

Chapter Eight

Asking for Help

If you met Brad, you might not guess he has a shy bone in his body. He greets you with a warm handshake, looks you in the eye without hesitation, and takes quick interest in finding out more about you. He has some close friends, teaches a junior-high Sunday-school class at church and is happily married. Indeed, in most areas Brad enjoys socializing and feels at home around people.

But there is one point in the world of interacting with people where his blood runs cold. He is terrified of job interviews. He approaches one with the same eagerness someone with vertigo feels over cleaning the gutters on a three-story house.

He never had to face his fear until six months ago. When he graduated from college, a job was waiting for him. A long-time family friend needed an editor for his small publishing house and felt that Brad, who excelled in his journalism major, would perform well. During his twelve years at this post Brad became proficient at editing and grew to love the work. But then the bottom fell out of his job situation. The owner of the firm died in a car accident, and his widow, unfamiliar with the publishing business and eager to move to a warmer climate, disbanded the company.

While Brad knew editing inside out, job-seeking was unfamiliar terrain and he felt like a sailor lost at sea. One thing he could do was write a good résumé. Even though his job experience was limited to this one firm, he described it on paper in a manner that would have impressed the president of IBM. An editor friend gave him a list of several hundred firms in Washington, D.C., which employed editors, and Brad mailed a copy of his résumé to each one. He scrupulously combed the papers for job openings and sent his résumé out at each opportunity. But after a month of this diligent paper pushing, he had not received a single call.

By now he had read enough job-seeking books to know exactly what he must do. He knew he had to make verbal inquiries of prospective employers. But for the life of him he just couldn't do it. It was embarrassing even to think of telling a receptionist over the phone that he needed work. He worried that he would get tongue-tied just asking for an interview. He worried that he would not be able to handle rejection—*any* rejection—even the polite response of a secretary that no positions are currently open.

And he worried incessantly about the interview itself: He was sure he would feel silly talking to someone else about his qualifications. And he wondered if he could stand up psychologically to the scrutiny of an unaffirming interviewer. Would he lose his train of thought, lapse into total panic and blank out? Would he be devastated beyond recovery if he wasn't offered the job?

For the next several weeks he went through the approach-avoidance behavior of a teenager trying to muster the courage to phone for his first date. He could not complete the many calls he tried to make, nor could he find the resolve to visit any firms in person. Finally, he was thrilled to receive a phone call from a company, offering him an interview. But he was so nervous on the morning it was scheduled that he left a message on their answering machine saying he was unable to keep the appointment. It was at this point that he realized he needed help.

Brad thought of Bob Foster, the new associate pastor at his church. Pastor Bob seemed approachable and had already shown an interest in Brad. For the past several Sundays he had told Brad he was praying for his job search, and last Sunday he had added that Brad should call him if he needed any help. Brad decided to accept his offer and tell him of his job-seeking phobia. Though he knew it would be embarrassing to admit to anyone that his fears ran as deep as they did, he felt it would be easier to talk about this with Pastor Bob than to go through an interview itself. This could be a beginning step.

Bob Foster did several things which helped Brad. He confessed to him that he, too, had worked through some similar fears when seeking his first church position. Brad was comforted to find that his struggles were not unique, as he had thought. The pastor assured Brad that he was not mentally ill but simply locked up in the inertia of some fears which could be confronted. He gave him some practical tips for handling his fear. In addition, he affirmed Brad and told him he was convinced he could survive an interview and find a suitable job. His confidence was reassuring to Brad.

But Bob Foster took one further step which made all the difference. He gave Brad accountability. "I'm going to sit on you," he said. "I want you to plan on making a minimum of ten phone calls a day requesting interviews until you get one. I also want you to phone me *every day* at five p.m. and report on your progress." Brad was startled by Pastor Bob's assertiveness but realized it could be just what the doctor ordered.

When Brad sat down the next morning to do his phoning, the first call was a frightening challenge. After a dozen attempts he still had not completed the number. But Brad remembered that he would be sharing his experience with Pastor Bob later that day. Eager to prove himself and buoyed up by remembering his pastor friend was praying for his success, he finally went through with the call. As it turned out, the conversation with the receptionist who answered was uneventful. She politely told Brad that there were no current openings but they would be happy to receive his résumé and keep his name in consideration.

When Brad hung up from that three-minute conversation, he felt as if he had scaled a ten-thousand-foot summit! Far from being discouraged by the inconclusiveness of the call, he was ecstatic simply to have completed it and still be in one piece. Pastor Bob was right, he *could* do it. Taking heart from this one success, he made the next nine calls in rapid order and then with time remaining made several more. At 5:00 he reported to Pastor Bob that while no one had offered an interview, several employers had requested his résumé and showed some signs of interest.

"You're on a roll, Brad. Keep it up!" the pastor responded.

For the next two days Brad continued the plan, making thirteen calls one day and fifteen the next. Each day it was a bit difficult completing the first call, but after that it was easier. By the end of the third day, though, there was still no specific offer of an interview, only indirect indications of interest.

But on the fourth day the phone rang before Brad began his routine. It was one of the offices he had phoned before—an aerospace association which had just received his résumé in the mail. "Your qualifications look promising," a friendly woman's voice announced. "Can you come in tomorrow morning for a consultation?"

"Yes," Brad responded, sounding excited but already feeling as if all the blood was draining out of his body.

Second Thoughts
For the rest of the day Brad obsessed about the ordeal facing him

the next morning. When he finally spoke with Pastor Bob at 5:00 he blurted out, "I have an interview tomorrow. This is a great accomplishment. But I just don't think I can go through with it. I feel like a lamb being led to the slaughter. I know I won't sleep a wink tonight."

"Brad," Bob Foster responded, "you must do it. Even if you faint or die on the spot, you must go through with this commitment. Think of it as emergency major surgery which, though it's frightening, is absolutely necessary to submit to. Besides, I know it won't seem even like minor surgery once you're into it. I know you'll do well. I *promise* you that you'll hold up just fine."

Once again Brad was heartened by his pastor's confidence. Taking the surgery analogy to heart, he decided to submit himself to the scalpel.

Several times the next morning Brad came close to phoning to cancel the interview. But, remembering Pastor Bob's urgings, he finally dragged himself to his car and drove to the high-rise where the office was located. He arrived just in time for the 10:00 appointment, took a few deep breaths and went in.

The interview lasted longer than Brad expected, almost an hour. After the first few minutes he felt surprisingly comfortable interacting with the middle-aged man who interviewed him. He found he actually enjoyed talking about his qualifications with this stranger. At the end of the interview the man told Brad that while he was impressed with his skills, he felt he should probably hire someone more familiar with the aerospace industry. He would, however, spread the word about Brad's availability among others he knew. Brad thanked him sincerely and walked out of the office.

Brad didn't wait for 5:00. He drove directly to the pastor's office. "I didn't get the job," Brad reported, "but I still feel like I've given birth. Simply completing that interview was the greatest accomplishment of my life."

During the next two weeks Brad netted three more interviews

from his phoning. In each case he phoned Bob Foster for prayer and encouragement to keep the appointment—but he found each one easier to handle. At the end of the fourth interview he was offered a position. The firm was a poultry association needing someone to supervise production of its monthly newsletter. Never mind that Brad couldn't tell a rooster from a goose. The employer was impressed with his literary skills and convinced he could learn enough about the business to fulfill the role effectively. Brad was delighted with the offer and accepted the job. Only a few weeks before, he had been sure this sort of position would never open up for him.

Help from Our Friends

I have seen the story repeated time and again. One person like Brad, who suffers from deep-seated fears in a certain area, is helped greatly by another who believes in him and acts as a coach or mentor in prodding him to move ahead. The direct interest which that person takes in his plight—the coaching, praying and cheering that person does—becomes the magic ingredient that inspires the shy person to confront his fear and to take steps which he once thought inconceivable. Brad's experience is not unusual.

I began this book with my own story of first trying to marshal the nerve to ask a young woman out. It was a genuinely traumatic episode for me as a young teenager. I credit one factor in my finally succeeding: the persistence of a friend in urging me—even nettling me—to make the call. The friend was a woman, several years my senior, who lived next door and was like an older sister to me. She took it on as her own personal crusade to see that I broke the barrier of shyness. And her crusade succeeded, in part because of her compassion, in part because of her tenacity. To the shy person a friend who takes on this role is a pearl of great price.

I benefited several years later from the encouragement of a

male friend who coached me through another challenging period when shyness again held me back from pursuing a relationship. Again his coaching was what gave me the incentive to break the ice.

In their work with phobia sufferers, Manuel Zane and Harry Milt actually require their clients to find someone to be a mentor to them throughout the time of recovery.[1] This person, whom Zane and Milt term the "helper," agrees to accompany the phobic person and encourage him or her in beginning to physically confront the fearful situation. As one example, they tell of a man with an extreme fear of darkness whose brother agreed to be his helper. His brother would stand alongside him as he stood in a totally darkened room for increasing periods of time, listening to him express his fears and reassuring him. The process worked well for this man, who in time overcame his phobia.

Indeed, it seems that God has fashioned us as humans to benefit in specific ways from another person's encouragement. Particularly when it comes to gaining courage, we are more likely to rise to the occasion if we know someone is standing with us. While there is plenty we can do by ourselves to confront our fears, and while prayer can work wonders, we benefit too from the direct support of another person. And as Brad's example suggests, such helpers can benefit us in a variety of important ways in the support relationship:

☐ *Through their identity with our struggle.* We are relieved to find that they also have fears and weaknesses; we feel less isolated.

☐ *Through their example.* We take heart from their personal success in confronting their fears.

☐ *Through their coaching.* They help us to develop a perspective for confronting our fears—a "track to run on."

☐ *Through their affirmation.* We benefit greatly just from their confidence that we can overcome our fears and from hearing them say, "You can do it!"

☐ *Through their prayers.* If this person is a Christian and committed to praying for us, an additional channel of spiritual power is now working for our benefit; we are encouraged to know this person is interceding for our success, and God will answer prayer by helping us in our struggle.

☐ *Through accountability.* By knowing there is someone keeping track of our successes and failures, we have a greater incentive to take steps forward. The point comes where it is therapeutic to have someone who "sits on us."

Once again, we do not have to look beyond Scripture to find examples where God used one person to impart courage to another.

Through meeting with his father-in-law, Moses gained perspective and courage to limit his response to people's back-breaking expectations and to delegate responsibility to others (Ex 18). Moses in turn was an agent of courage to Joshua and spoke emphatically to him of God's support in the excruciating responsibilities facing the young leader (Deut 31:7-8). David and Jonathan's friendship is well known and was a source of courage to them both on many occasions. Naomi gave incentive to Ruth to take bold steps to make herself available for marriage with Boaz (Ruth 3). Through consulting with her adoptive father, Mordecai, Esther gained the courage to take the life-threatening step of appearing before the king unannounced to plead for mercy on the Jews (Esther 4:4-17). Paul propped up Timothy on many occasions, and Timothy's friendship often gave fresh heart to Paul. Even Jesus himself seemed to gain special support from his relationship with Peter, James and John. The list goes on and on.

Both Scripture and experience suggest that we each can benefit significantly from a mentor in our efforts to overcome the inhibitions of shyness. Look closely at this possibility and carefully consider whether there is someone among your friends and acquaintances who could fulfill this role. In confronting fears of any nature it is an excellent idea to ask for help.

The Challenge of Asking for Help

This fact, though, leaves many of us who are shy in a proverbial catch-22. Asking for help means opening ourselves to a vulnerable relationship with someone; yet it is close encounters with people that we fear in the first place! It may seem that taking the initiative to ask someone to be our mentor would be as difficult as any other step we dread to take with people.

From experience, though, I find that this is not likely to be the case. Many of us find that among our pool of acquaintances there is someone who logically and naturally can fulfill this role. In some cases we are fortunate to have someone actually offer to help us. In other cases there is someone whom we feel more comfortable sharing with than most, and we find it possible to open up to them about our need for support in overcoming shyness.

Asking for help is a particularly manageable option for those of us who, like Brad, are shy in one but not all areas. Many of us are frightened only about a certain type of encounter with people, such as going through a job interview, seeking a date or a romantic relationship, or speaking before a crowd. In this case, it is not so frightening to ask someone who is outside of that situation to support us. While it may sting a bit to admit our need for help, asking for the assistance of an acquaintance is still easier than facing the situation we fear. It is a logical first step in confronting the situation.

Even those of us who are more generally shy often find it easier to ask someone to help us in combating shyness than to make the effort to initiate other types of relationships. One reason it is easier is the complete level of honesty involved in asking for help. There is no role-playing here, the mask is off, pretense is gone, and we are simply laying our life before someone as it is—what you see is what you get. This can be an easier step to take than other encounters with people where a higher level of social skill is needed.

Keep in mind, too, that the person who helps you does not necessarily have to be a close friend or peer, nor does this person have to be similar to you in age, culture or life experience. The only requirement is that they want to help you, believe in you and have the personality and gifts needed to support you. Beyond friends whom you are already close with, possibilities of someone who might fulfill the role are—

☐ A grandparent
☐ A brother or sister
☐ A parent or stepparent
☐ An aunt, uncle or cousin
☐ A neighbor
☐ A teacher who is affirming to you and has taken an interest in you as a person
☐ A pastor, youth director or church staff member
☐ An elder, deacon, Sunday-school teacher, Stephens Ministry member or other individual at your church
☐ A Bible-study leader, IVCF staffer or other spiritual leader whom you know
☐ The mother or father of a friend
☐ A family doctor (works in some cases where the traditional intimacy still exists)
☐ A professional counselor

How to Do It

Survey the options among the people you know and see if there isn't someone whom you can ask to be a mentor to you in your effort to overcome shyness. Pray earnestly that God will provide such a person for you and make clear to you if there is someone you should ask. Once you settle on someone, approach them specifically about being your helper. Ask to meet with them, or write them a letter explaining your situation. Tell them that you have suffered from shyness which has kept you from doing many things you want to do and caused you to miss out on a lot. Explain that you have decided to take some determined steps to get beyond the inhibiting effects of shyness and that you believe you will benefit from having someone stand with you in this effort. Ask them if they would be willing to help you decide on specific steps you can take and if they will stay in touch with you about your progress. If they are Christian, ask if they will agree to pray regularly for your healing and success. And tell them you need all the advice and encouragement they are willing to give.

Pray that God will give the person whom you ask wisdom in responding to your request. If perchance they tell you that they cannot be available for this role, don't feel rejected. It may well be that even though they would like to help you they are simply overcommitted at this time. Trust that God will provide help for you through someone else. Enjoy the fact that you found the courage to take this step. Realize that someone else's response may be quite different, and be willing to try again.

Chances are good, though, that you will get a positive response. Remember that many people are eager for the opportunity to help others. They want to know that their lives are accomplishing something worthwhile and benefiting others in specific ways. They are flattered to be asked to fulfill this sort of role and enjoy the opportunity considerably. Pray carefully, look carefully, and try to find someone who fits this description. If you choose the right person, you will not be a burden but a blessing to them.

Other Options

There is another option to the individual mentor which works well for some of us, and that is having a group play this same role. Some find that it is less intimidating to ask a group for help than a single individual, especially if the group has a supportive emphasis by definition. Bible studies, prayer groups and support groups in churches are often designed in part to be a forum where individuals can share their hurts and concerns and receive support from the other members. If you are in such a group or can join one, take advantage of the special opportunity for support which it affords. Share honestly with this group that you are shy. Ask for their prayers, advice, encouragement and "monitoring." Decide on some strategy with them for overcoming your fears, and ask them to hold you accountable for taking these steps.

By the way, you will probably be encouraged to find that others in the group will be inspired by your honesty to open up and share about their own fears. The camaraderie of this sharing can be reinforcing for all of you.

Joan Guest, in her booklet *Self-Esteem,* tells how she learned to deal with serious stage fright in performing with the harp by sharing frankly about her fears with a support group of Christian friends. The knowledge that they accepted her for who she was and the confidence that they were praying for her, while not fully annulling her fears, did give her the measure of faith she needed to rise above them. She found it possible to perform again.[2]

There are other support group options that work very well for some, including shyness support groups, twelve-step and codependency groups, and professional organizations for developing public speaking skills such as Toastmasters. I will look more closely at each of these options in chapter ten. I will also offer further advice on finding the best group opportunities for developing friendships and relationships. Keep in mind that sometimes the goal of getting help and the goal of making friends can be met in the same setting.

Do I Need Professional Help?

Any discussion of asking for help invariably raises the question of whether we who are shy would benefit from professional counseling. You may wonder if you are suffering from the sort of problem which requires long-term therapy or an ongoing relationship with a counselor. This is a perplexing question for some shy persons and a troubling one for others.

Let me relieve you quickly in saying that simply being shy does not mean you are mentally ill, emotionally disturbed or in any sort of state which would necessarily require a psychologist or professional counselor. Shyness in itself is a phobia, and as we have said, a phobia is a learned response of fear which is usually cured not through analyzing but through experience. The best remedy for any phobia is actual experience confronting what we fear, which gradually acclimates us to the frightening situation and brings us to the point of being comfortable in it. Shyness is healed, or at least managed, by successful experiences functioning in the social situations which intimidate us. Any assistance from another person which helps us gain the courage to step into these situations we fear will help us considerably in the healing process. That help can come from a psychologist or professional counselor. But it can also come from our pastor or the neighbor next door. Our major need is for someone to encourage us to move forward and to hold us accountable for doing so.

Generally I recommend long-term counseling only if it is clear that there are problems other than basic shyness hindering you from getting involved with people or from realizing your potential. If, for instance, you were raised in an abusive family situation, you may have been emotionally wounded on several fronts: in addition to shyness you may be suffering from repressed anger toward your parents and from chronically low self-esteem. These factors will aggravate the shy tendencies which you have. In this case, counseling can help you considerably to come to terms with your past, to learn to express your feelings appropriately, and to develop a more healthy self-image.

Even *with* such counseling, though, you will still need positive social experiences that help you to break the shyness barrier. You may still benefit from a person or group in addition to your counselor who plays the mentor role.

If your family background has been generally healthy, or if your shyness has grown out of an overprotective upbringing, your major need is probably not to analyze your past but to break the inertia which shyness imposes on you. Here I would not recommend in-depth counseling, though it may be that a counselor with a directive approach could act as a coach or mentor to help you break that inertia.

Different Approaches

Counselors do vary considerably in the approaches that they take. Some follow an analytical, pschotherapeutic approach, which involves digging into the past and identifying the root of emotional problems. Often such counselors are very nondirective, preferring to ask you questions which prod you to reach conclusions on your own. Other counselors are more directive; they are not hesitant to give detailed advice and may put more emphasis on what you need to do to get out of the pit than upon trying to discover how you got there. Many Christian counselors try to strike a balance between these extremes, giving some attention to analyzing but some real emphasis to straightforward advice as well.

If you are dealing with problems rooted in a difficult upbringing, you will probably benefit from a counselor who takes a psychotherapeutic approach. I personally know many people out of such backgrounds who have benefited greatly from a long-term relationship with this type of counselor. At the other extreme you may simply need someone who will give you a pep talk and some gentle encouragement to move forward. Again, that help may come from a counselor with a directive approach or from anyone else who has the gifts to help you. If you are not certain what your counseling needs are, visit a counselor and ask them to advise you on whether you would benefit from a series of sessions or an ongoing counseling relationship. Be very upfront in asking this counselor to tell you what their philosophy of counseling is and to give you an honest opinion as to whether that approach is really what you need.

And don't be afraid to get second opinions. Pastors, too, are often well equipped to advise you about the possibility of professional counseling. Get the best help you can; but be sure it is help you really need. Remember that ultimately you must take responsibility for your own life. The shyness problem is one of inertia that must be broken, and you are the only one who can finally step through that barrier. Look for the sort of relationship with a friend, acquaintance or counselor which best helps you do that.

Part Three

Awakening Your Social Life

Chapter Nine

Seeing the Possibilities

One of the most delightful qualities of young children is their conviction that life is full of marvelous surprises which are simply awaiting discovery. When my young boys visit my parents' old twelve-room home, they spend long periods rummaging around the cavernous attic looking for hidden treasure. They never lose their conviction that some priceless relic is to be found in the next unexplored pile of artifacts or the next unopened box.

In fact, they do sometimes strike gold. Recently they found my Georgetown University yearbook from 1966, a volume I'd long forgotten. On page 174 is a photo of a young man with the caption "President Bill Clinton." Yes, it is *the* Bill Clinton. And, yes, I did say the year was 1966. He was a second-year student at Georgetown at the time and president of the sophomore class. There he is in all his glory, standing slightly slouched, immediately recognizable, looking only slightly less self-assured than at present, in a photo that is eerily prophetic. Thanks to my boys' optimistic exploration, Evie and I now have an interesting conversation piece for our living room.

As we come into our adult years, we tend to lose the optimistic expectations of youth, and this can be tragic. When it comes to social life, for instance, many people think they are aware of all the possibilities for meeting people where they live. They don't imagine life has any surprises waiting for them in this area. But the best options for social life often are not very apparent. They certainly do not announce themselves with neon lights. People who are well informed in other areas can be amazingly unaware of excellent social opportunities available under their very noses.

Surprising Discoveries

For example, I did not discover the youth and college ministry programs of Fourth Presbyterian Church in Washington, D.C., until I was nineteen years old. I grew up only a few miles from the church, and my family belonged to the country club directly across the street from it. Though I spent many summer days at the club's pool—and never made a friend in the process—it didn't even cross my mind that there might be golden opportunities for friendship at the church across the street. The irony continues in that I was introduced to Fourth not by anyone in my area but by visitors from out of town whom I met on a summer job. They invited me to visit the church and I did so—once. It was not until a year later that I made a return visit and at that time discovered the college ministry.

I was amazed to find an active, dynamic group of about sixty college students, where the friendship and Christian love shown to me surpassed anything I had experienced to that point in my life. Within a few years the group grew to several hundred. It was here that I made many lasting friendships, developed a music ministry and by God's grace met my wife. The involvement in Fourth's college ministry enriched and broadened my life in innumerable ways. Of even greater importance was the spiritual nurture I received during that time. Yet I almost missed this life-changing opportunity that was virtually on my doorstep.

In the same way Evie and I were surprised and delighted to discover the ministry of Montgomery Methodist Church in the country town of Damascus, Maryland, where we now live. As you drive around the Damascus region you pass an infinite number of Methodist churches (well, twenty to be exact), and most seem to fit the stereotype—small but pretty edifices adjoining a cemetery where the multitude of gravestones quickly tells you that the deceased members of the congregation greatly outnumber the living. A visit with the living membership typically reveals a cordial but tiny congregation which has little activity outside of the Sunday service. Not exactly a fertile environment for making new friends, you might conclude.

A person might assume this stereotype fits all of the Methodist churches, or even all of the churches in our region, and never bother looking for a more dynamic worshiping community. Yet on the north side of Damascus, tucked away in the woods, is a large Methodist church building not even visible from the highway. Inside on Sundays a thriving congregation of over five hundred meets and enjoys solid evangelical teaching from Rev. Mark Derby, who has pastored the church for over a decade. There are many subgroups within the church, including one of the strongest men's fellowships in our county. The quality of friendships within the church is strong, and the love extended to newcomers is warm and genuine. It is an excellent environment for spiritual growth and for meeting other Christians.

Yet most people I meet who live within commuting distance of this church are unaware of its existence. That's the way it is with some of the best social and spiritual opportunities! Churches and fellowship groups generally do little or no advertising. Word-of-mouth advertising is rare, for most people fear treading on your privacy and so do not tell you about their favorite church or group. Most surprising is the lack of communication among churches themselves, even churches of the same denomination. I am often amazed to find how little members of one congregation know about the activities of other churches only a short distance away.

Even the most dynamic and unusual opportunities can escape our notice. Fourth Presbyterian now fosters a huge career singles group of about five hundred, the Ambassadors. Their activities include a well-organized and creative Sunday-school program. Yet I constantly talk with singles in the Washington area who are eager to find such a fellowship, yet have no idea that the group exists.

Often the best opportunities are found only by careful exploration, and with persistence not unlike that of my boys looking for treasures in their grandparents' attic. Don't be too quick to think that you are acquainted with all of the good options in the area where you live.

Broadening Our Vision
We can miss, too, excellent opportunities for meeting people within a reasonable commuting distance of where we live. If you do not live within the immediate boundaries of a major metropolitan area, you may well be within a one- to two-hour drive of one. This is not too far to drive to a church or social gathering, if the setting is one which meets your needs particularly well.

The trade-off is especially reasonable if your daily commute to work is not long. Many people in the region where I live negotiate bumper-to-bumper traffic for an hour or two each direction to work. Understandably, they are not eager to drive great distances to church or social activities. But if your job is close to your home and you enjoy driving or are near public transportation, look seriously at the possibility of making a long-distance run for your fellowship opportunities.

What a Difference a Change Makes
We also tend to underestimate the positive effect a change in

setting—sometimes even a simple change—can have on our social life. We should not assume that the way others relate to us will be the same in every setting. Every social group is different and has its own personality. Substantial differences will exist from group to group in how others respond to you. As I visit different churches, I am often struck with how moving from one church to another is like moving to a different city. This can be true even with churches in the same neighborhood or on the same block. In one you are stigmatized or ignored; but then in the church down the street you are warmly accepted and treated with positive expectations.

Recently a single woman in her early thirties told me how she had been actively involved in a large church singles group for seven years but never been asked on a date. Finally, with some reluctance, she left and became active in a smaller singles fellowship in a church not far away. Within a short time several different men were expressing an interest in dating her. This change may be due in part to differences in her own attitude in the new situation. Yet I suspect the new setting was one that worked more to her advantage. I have seen this pattern repeated many times.

The lesson is that we should not automatically assume that our experience will be the same in every social setting. Change can sometimes make all the difference.

The Unparalleled Benefits of Christian Fellowship

I find, too, that many Christians undervalue or even become numb to the exceptional benefits which the Christian fellowship environment provides for building friendships and relationships. I am particularly alert to the stark differences between Christian and secular social settings, not having become a Christian until age nineteen. I was, in fact, astounded to discover the Christian fellowship setting and to find how fully I was accepted by others—apart from any effort to prove myself. The contrast with my previous social experiences was so striking that I have never ceased being thankful for it.

Your success in a secular social setting often depends upon how well you impress others through your physical presence, your talents or social skills. While these qualities can work to your advantage in Christian fellowship as well, they do not take on the same all-or-nothing importance. And too often your acceptance in the secular social scene depends upon a quality or skill which may not be natural to you.

The most pervasive secular social activity remains dancing. While I am not opposed to most dancing from any spiritual or moral standpoint, I am painfully aware of how the dancing environment is usually one in which it is difficult for the shy person to come off well. You are put on public display in so many ways at a dance. You must either take the mortifying step of asking someone to be your partner or wait helplessly for someone to ask you to dance. The fact that others are watching not only adds to your mortification if you are refused or not asked, but magnifies your fear of asking someone to dance in the first place.

If your request is accepted, your partner and others quickly discover just how skilled you are at dancing. And, of course, here is the catch-22. Most often the shy person lacks dancing experience and thus is something less than an Arthur Murray professional. If you are dancing with a stranger, that person's first impression of you is your dancing ability. Even if the person is able to see beyond your ox-footedness to appreciate the true person inside, you are likely to be so self-conscious about your dancing effort that the relationship never gets off the ground.

There is also an immediate and forced intimacy in the dancing situation which is unnerving for many shy people. Yet for the person wanting to meet people of the opposite sex in a secular setting, it can seem that dancing provides one of the best opportunities, even that it is an unavoidable necessity.

When I read Philip Zimbardo's classic *Shyness,* I was struck with how often he gives readers advice about how to function effectively at a dance. The advice he gives is good. But the underlying message is that if you want to win friends and influence people—and especially if you want to find a serious relationship—you need to be able to do well in the dancing environment. As I read his remarks I could only feel sympathy for those shy people who must negotiate the social maze without the benefit of Christian fellowship. And I was reminded how fortunate we Christians are to have a setting where we can become successful, full-functioning social beings apart from any dancing skills.

My point is not to take a backhanded swat at Christians who like to dance. Some Christians enjoy dancing, are talented at it and find it helps them to meet people. There is also an increasing tendency among Christian singles groups to sponsor dances. All of this is fine. My point is simply that we do not need to be skilled at dancing or anything else to be successful in the Christian social environment. Our relationship with Christ in itself gives an immediate point of identity and allows us to begin from a position of strength in any relationship with other Christians.

This is not to say that the only decent social opportunities for us are within Christian fellowship. There can be excellent opportunities in secular settings as well. But we should not lose sight of the advantages we have as Christians. In the next chapter we will look more closely at how we can find the best opportunities in either the Christian or secular context for enhancing our social life.

Chapter Ten

Putting Yourself
in the Right Context

Recently a woman shared with me an encouraging account of how she overcame teenage shyness. Lisa was so uncomfortable with people during her school years that she stuck to herself and had few friends. Even when riding the school bus, she seldom spoke with anyone.

Things changed dramatically when she went away to college. She enrolled in a Nazarene college several hundred miles from her home. Once there, she made the pleasant discovery that her new classmates, who knew nothing of her past, did not instinctively label her as shy, as folks at home had done. People on campus were friendly to her and invited her to school activities. This buoyed her confidence and she began to take more initiative with others in return.

In her third year of college she decided to fight her shyness aggressively. "I got involved in every activity I possibly could, especially for the opportunity to meet people," she said. As she grew comfortable relating to people in one situation, it became easier in other settings as well.

Then she took a particularly courageous step. She agreed to go on a summer missions trip with a group of students whom she did not know. The team visited poor communities in California and presented the gospel to underprivileged children through puppet shows. Her responsibility included knocking on doors and inviting perfect strangers to attend. In town after town, she made the gratifying discovery that people did not bite her hand off but accepted her warmly. The whole experience increased her confidence with people remarkably.

Now, at twenty-seven, she is an office manager and active in the singles group of her church. I have spoken at two events Lisa attended, one a weekend retreat, and in each case I was impressed with her congeniality and how she extended herself to others. She is well liked and accepted by others in the group.

An Inspiring Example

I look at Lisa as an encouraging model of how the tide can turn for any of us who are shy. She took several steps which helped her break the inertia of shyness. Going *away* to college was an important move. She was accepted, not stigmatized as shy. She responded well and became more outgoing. It helped, too, that she chose a small college where the social climate was more friendly and inclusive than is often the case at a larger university.

Deciding to join the summer missions team was a particularly smart move. Through the constant adjustment to new situations, she discovered that people were approachable wherever she went, and this broke her of the fear of making new acquaintances. She also received training for meeting people door-to-door, and the skills she gained in relating to people have helped her in other situations.

Lisa's example shows how our social life can benefit from changes in our circumstances. It reminds us that if we are serious about overcoming the inhibitions of shyness, we need to put ourselves in the best situations for this to happen. We don't necessarily have to take steps as radical as she did, in order to jump-start our social life. There may be excellent opportunities in our own area we haven't yet discovered. While a major move may sometimes be the best step, making changes where we are can make a big difference as well.

We need to be bold and creative in seeking the best situations for improving our social life. How, then, do we find these? There are many types of social situations where our various needs can be met, and it is important to be aware of the options. Before looking at those, though, it is important to know how to judge whether a particular social situation is right for us.

Judging the Context
How do I know whether a group or activity is appropriate to my needs as a shy person? Lisa made strides because she exercised good judgment in the situations that she chose. Making wise choices is no small challenge. Yet there are principles which can help. Here are eight guidelines which can help us judge the benefits of a social situation we are in or a new opportunity that comes along.

1. Is the potential strong in this setting for making friends with others who hold my values? I cannot assume that, simply because I am a Christian, God will automatically provide friendships with others who hold my convictions. The responsibility rests in part with me, particularly in terms of judging a social situation for its merits. It is naive, for instance, to think that I will find a healthy friendship or relationship at a singles bar or similar scene. My time is valuable, and the few precious hours I have for investing in social life should be given to situations with the highest potential for producing quality relationships.

2. Is the situation an affirming one? It is no secret that some social environments are more accepting and affirming than others. This is as true in Christian communities as anywhere else. In some churches, for instance, individuals are belittled for sins and failings and even put on public display. In others there is a much greater emphasis upon the forgiveness and grace of Christ. In choosing a church or fellowship group, look for one with a strongly grace-centered emphasis. Look for one, too, where the members themselves are outgoing and encouraging to others, particularly newcomers.

3. Am I likely to be valued as an individual in this setting, and will my gifts be appreciated? A closely related concern is how much value a group places upon individual distinctiveness. Many churches and Christian organizations have rigidly objective standards by which they judge the value of an individual's service to Christ, and the message which comes across is that all Christians should serve the Lord in basically the same way. It may be taught that all believers are expected to be aggressive evangelists, or church recruiters, or exercise a certain spiritual gift. In other Christian settings, great respect is held for the uniqueness of the individual. It is recognized that God has made us each different, has given us radically different gifts and personality features, and has unique areas of service for each of us. Look for situations with this emphasis.

And look for those where the particular gifts you do have are most likely to be needed and welcomed. If you have a talent for leading praise music, for instance, it would probably be unwise to sink your time into a group which does not value contemporary forms of worship.

4. Are the prospects good for meeting members of the opposite sex? If you are eager for marriage or to find a serious relationship, be sure some of your activities provide good opportunity for meeting Christians of the opposite sex. Churches and parachurch ministries often encourage same-sex activities (men's prayer breakfasts, women's Bible studies), and these can be beneficial in many ways. During the time of your life when you are actively exploring the possibility of marriage, though, you should consider it a point of stewardship to place yourself in the very best settings for meeting someone suitable to marry. This should not be thought of as forcing the hand of God, but as taking mature responsibility for your life as a Christian.

If your singles group sponsors both same-sex and mixed Bible studies, for instance, and your schedule will only allow you to attend one, choose the mixed study. Remember that next to deciding to follow Christ, the marriage decision is the most far-reaching choice you will make in this life. And Christian fellowship groups generally provide the best setting for meeting someone who could become your spouse. Don't deprive yourself of this opportunity simply because it seems more spiritual to spend time with members of your own sex. Allow some balance in this area, and take advantage of the best opportunities available for building opposite-sex friendships.

5. Is there healthy membership growth in this group? This too is an important consideration if you are single and interested in marriage. Some church singles groups are small, even ingrown, and may go for months or years with little change in membership. Your prospects for finding someone to marry are better in a group where new people visit and become involved on a regular basis. Be sure the group you align with is large enough and dynamic enough to allow for this momentum. This doesn't mean it has to be the monstrous size of the Ambassadors of Fourth Presbyterian. A group of thirty to sixty singles can be one which attracts newcomers, if it is in a dynamic and growing church. Use your best judgment, and select a group with a future.

6. Have I become stigmatized in this group? This is one of the most difficult questions we have to confront, yet from time to time we need to face it. As we noted, labeling occurs in every social setting. Usually it goes on innocently, with no malicious intent. Yet over time, people form impressions of us which do not easily change.

If you have been involved in a singles group for two or three years, for instance, and no one has shown interest in dating you, it may be that others are now thinking of you as a permanent single. It is not that this impression cannot possibly change, and determined action on your part may help to change it. Yet it is still a default mode in your relationship with this group—one with which you must reckon.

Sometimes, simply moving to a different group can make a big difference. Since people in the new situation do not have a predefined view of you, you have the chance to establish a fresh identity. A different momentum may take place with dating, and others may show more interest in getting to know you. Change for change's sake can be a good idea at times, especially if you consider it prayerfully and carefully weigh the options. Don't rule it out or be afraid to face the possibility that some stigmatizing has occurred in your current situation. It happens to all of us.

7. *Will this situation challenge me to venture out of my shell?* While it is important that the social settings you choose are affirming ones, it is also desirable that they are ones which challenge you to extend yourself and to break the barriers of shyness. This can be an important consideration in choosing a job. Many shy Christians tell me that they have benefited from being in a job which requires them to be outgoing or assertive. Though at first they felt like a frightened parachutist being pushed from a plane, in time the pressure proved to be exactly what they needed to gain greater confidence and effectiveness with people.

Belinda, who was plagued with chronic shyness growing up, remarks, "I am a teacher's aide at a high school, working with a lot of students who are learning-disabled. My job as an aide puts me in front of a lot of people, often speaking and teaching, and that experience has helped me get over my shyness. It also helps to know that what I'm doing is important."

Aram, a fifty-nine-year-old Presbyterian pastor, comments, "Being a pastor has forced me to be assertive. I used to hate to speak before people. Now I love to preach, even though I'm nervous every Sunday until I get started."

Others note that jobs requiring them to sell, to supervise people or to make presentations to groups have helped them significantly. In choosing a job, carefully consider how it will help you in overcoming shyness. The dividends from such on-the-job training with people can be enormous.

In choosing a church or fellowship group, too, look carefully at whether you will be challenged to minister to people in this setting or whether your involvement will more likely be that of a spectator. Again, I have the testimony of many Christians, like Lisa, who were drawn out of their protective wrapping through getting involved in ministry opportunities provided by churches and Christian organizations. These include leadership roles, musical and dramatic opportunities, evangelism projects and numerous other areas of service. Look for those settings in the body of Christ where you will be challenged to reach out to others and given effective ways to do it.

It is likewise important to consider whether a situation offers good role models. When Paul wrote the Philippians from prison, he noted, "Now I want you to know, brothers, that what has happened to me has really served to advance the gospel. . . . Because of my chains, most of the brothers in the Lord have been encouraged to speak the word of God more courageously and fearlessly" (Phil 1:12, 14). Paul's courage in standing up to the hardships of prison inspired many other Christians to be courageous in the challenges they faced. The confidence or cowardice which others around us display affects us profoundly. I am more likely to find the courage to go down the ski slope if the woman ahead of me confidently pushes off than if she has second thoughts and walks away.

In the same way we benefit from being around those who set a good example in their manner of relating to people. Look for situations which provide good role models and allow yourself to be inspired by the positive examples these people provide. It is particularly inspiring to be around shy people who have made progress in overcoming their inhibitions. We take heart from their success and are encouraged to be more outgoing.

8. *Beware of unrealistic ideals.* It is unlikely that any one social situation will match up perfectly with all of these standards. It is more realistic to hope that your overall *mix* of social activities will accomplish these goals, at least in a reasonable way. Beware, though, of overly perfectionistic standards in judging any social setting. Social life, by definition, means interacting with human creatures who by nature have plenty of failings. And God will use even the best social situation not only to encourage you but to challenge you—by helping you learn to love others who, like yourself, fall well short of perfect. Generally speaking, short of outright abusive or demoralizing situations, any social life is better than none. Still, your goal should be to look for the *best* opportunities available.

Making Choices

With these guidelines in mind, let's look more closely at the main opportunities for meeting people and note how we can best benefit from them.

The church context. While the church setting generally provides the best situation we have as Christians for building friendships and relationships, we will reap its benefits only if we take advantage of the special fellowship opportunities it provides. The Sunday service, usually the most important part of a church's ministry, is not in itself particularly conducive to meeting people. Some churches do feature worship services with a relational emphasis, and many services have a brief interlude for shaking hands and greeting those around you. Yet the mood of the worship service is still strongly controlled by our Western tradition of respecting the privacy of individuals and their right to commune with God in the solitude of their own hearts.

This is as it should be. Yet we must be honest in recognizing that the very factors in the worship environment which inspire individual devotion make it all too easy for a shy person to attend church—even regularly—and never meet a soul. There are many who faithfully worship at their local parish from the cradle to the grave, yet never make a meaningful friendship or learn anything significant about the hurts or needs of those worshiping around them. Fortunately, in many churches an effort is made to phone or visit newcomers and encourage them to take part in other activities. You should not assume this will happen, however. When you visit a church or call for information, carefully inquire about the Sunday school, adult or young adult fellowship, small groups and subgroup activities. Make sure you talk with someone who is in a position to know about all of the activities going on. In a larger church, many laypeople—even active ones—may not be aware of some of the programs taking place. You'll do best to talk with a pastor, staff member or church secretary.

It is the Sunday school and fellowship groups of a church that provide you with the golden opportunities for making new friends. Try to find a church that offers both solid biblical teaching *and* good opportunities for fellowship. Choose the church that offers a Sunday-school class or fellowship group for people of your age range and general life experience. Then visit this group. You may feel uneasy making the first visit. Yet I urge you to "feel the fear and do it anyway." Chances are good you will have a gratifying experience, and subsequent visits will be *much* easier after that initial effort of breaking the ice.

Again, churches differ. Take advantage of the magnificent freedom of movement we enjoy in American society to visit different churches and subgroups until you find a setting that is right for you. Simply keep in mind that you will not find a perfect situation. Look instead for a *suitable* setting and one that seems to be the best available in your area. Then cease your exploration and plant your feet with these people. Commitment and faithful attendance will be absolutely necessary to reap the benefits which are available.

It is possible, though, to be actively involved with more than one church, particularly as far as the subgroups are concerned. A large number of singles who attend the Ambassadors Sunday-school class at Fourth Presbyterian at 9:00 a.m., for instance, worship elsewhere at 11:00. While many attending the Ambassadors class do choose to align with Fourth, the church puts no pressure on singles to change their church membership, but regards Ambassadors as an outreach ministry. This makes it possible for one to be actively involved with Ambassadors but maintain a commitment to a home church.

You may find many possibilities like this. The Saturday morning men's breakfast at the Episcopal church may provide an ideal fellowship opportunity, while you maintain your commitment to worship on Sunday mornings at the Baptist church. Such options can usually be found with some careful exploration. Be creative in looking for the best mix of opportunities available in your area—or within a reasonable commute of where you live.

Parachurch ministries. Numerous outreach and fellowship-oriented ministries operate outside the framework of the local church. In my area, "First Monday Night" is a large and vibrant singles ministry not directly associated with any specific church or denomination. It features an outreach meeting on the first Monday evening of each month held in a hotel ballroom (the "Main Event"), as well as numerous support groups, retreats and special events. Other parachurch ministries in the Washington area include well-organized Bible studies for women (Community Bible Study, Bible Study Fellowship) and various men's organizations such as Christian Businessmen's Fellowship.

Discovering options like these can be more of a challenge than finding church opportunities, for such ministries seldom advertise, and even informed Christians often are not aware of their existence. But pastors frequently are, particularly those who oversee active evangelical churches. Most pastors are quite approachable and happy to tell you what they know about activities available in their area. Make it a point to phone a dozen or so pastors and ask them to fill you in on parachurch activities they know about which relate to your needs. You may uncover some surprising options. Be sure, though, to ask a number of pastors for their advice, for some will be aware of the good opportunities while others will not. Remember that there is wisdom in a multitude of counselors.

The school context. Though in terms of a lifetime we spend only a small fraction of time in the college environment, the campus setting provides unparalleled opportunities for meeting people and developing interpersonal skills. In college you are always starting off with a clean slate, among people who know little or nothing about your past; this is true even if you attend college near your home. As Lisa's experience reminds us, this fresh start can be therapeutic in many ways. And within the college setting are numerous clubs, athletic and musical organizations, and social activities where you have the potential for making friends.

There are usually exceptional opportunities in college—even the secular university—for meeting other Christians. Groups such as InterVarsity Christian Fellowship, Campus Crusade for Christ and Navigators hold regular meetings and offer small-group Bible studies. Most colleges have indigenous Christian ministries as well, often sponsored by the chaplaincy, and denominational groups such as Baptist Student Union.

If you are currently a student, treasure your situation for the unique opportunities for Christian fellowship it provides. Inquire at the student activities office, search the school newspaper and bulletin boards for announcements, and ask the chaplain for advice on activities. You will certainly find some which are worth visiting, and chances are good you will find a prize situation for growing in Christ and developing Christian relationships.

Missions, social service ministries and projects. More than a few shy people have told me that they were helped greatly by participating in a mission or service project which required them to extend themselves to others. An abundance of summer and short-term missions projects take place each year in our country and abroad. As Lisa's involvement with the puppet ministry brings out, these can be life-changing experiences. Pastors are often aware of opportunities and can put you in touch with mission boards which offer them. Campus organizations such as InterVarsity Christian Fellowship sponsor excellent opportunities and can apprise you of options outside of their organization as well.

It is hard to go anywhere in the United States today, whether in rural or metropolitan areas, where you do not find special missions directed to helping homeless and destitute people. These are sponsored by churches, governmental agencies and independent groups. Phoning some local churches should quickly uncover their existence. Consider offering your time to help with one of these enterprises. You will not only provide some invaluable assistance to fellow humans who are suffering; you will stretch yourself in some important ways as well. The prospects for meeting other Christians through this service are good, for even secular missions to the destitute tend to attract Christian workers.

Self-help support groups. If your shyness is rooted in an abusive family background, you can find help not only through counseling but through involvement in support groups. Such groups as Al-Anon (for children of alcoholics), which is patterned on the twelve-step model of Alcoholics Anonymous, are in abundant supply around the United States today. Many churches also sponsor them, sometimes under the name "Ephesians 5:15." They provide both a healing environment for coming to terms with past wounds and a forum for meeting others and learning to be assertive. There is also catharsis in discovering that others have come from backgrounds similar to your own—and that others wrestle with chronic shyness. You are inspired by the role models of those who have overcome their inhibitions.

Support groups *specifically* for shy people exist also, though these are not in as great supply as codependency programs. But it is well worth keeping an eye open for them. Their meetings may be announced in small ads in local newspapers. Local hospitals and mental health organizations may also be aware of them or even sponsor them; phone and ask for information. If a shyness support group is available where you live, by all means visit it and see if it is a setting where you can find help.

For those who want to conquer public-speaking anxieties, polish presentation skills or simply increase their confidence with people, Toastmasters, which sponsors some 7,000 chapters nationwide, provides an exceptional opportunity for personal growth. Members who attend the monthly meetings are given the opportunity to make brief speeches to an empathetic and supportive audience, many who are public-speaking phobics themselves. Through encouragement and coaching, individuals are nudged beyond their anxieties and helped to gain assurance and competence in front of a group. Several shy Christians have sung the praises of Toastmasters to me and said that this group has given them the boost they needed. If this sounds like an option that would be helpful to you, check your phone directory to see if there is a Toastmasters chapter near where you live.

Other options. In every city or community there are organizations for individuals with specific skills or interests. These include athletic leagues, dramatic and musical organizations, professional associations, clubs for collectors and hobbyists of every sort, and unique organizations such as the Izaak Walton League bird-watching society. If you have a skill or creative interest or the desire to develop one, you will undoubtedly find an organized group of like-minded souls in your area who would be delighted for you to join their company. This can be an excellent setting for the shy person to gain social confidence, for you already have an advantage in the common interest you share with others in the group. Give this option some consideration, and if the shoe fits, look carefully for an organized activity you would enjoy participating in and become part of it.

Making a Major Move

I have spoken mainly in this chapter about looking for opportunities to expand your social life in the area where you live. But what about pulling up stakes and moving to a different area where the opportunities are more abundant? Lisa's example of going away to college reminds us that the benefits of a major move can be considerable.

Every six months or so, take inventory of your life. Take a comfortable period of time—a Saturday morning or Sunday afternoon perhaps—and in a leisurely and prayerful spirit, examine the major circumstances in your life. Are there factors which are not helping you or are even working against your reaching important goals? Are your horizons limited in areas such as friendships, spiritual growth, personal education, career opportunities and, yes, even finding marriage? If so, then carefully consider how you can improve or change these circumstances. Do not hesitate to consider major changes, such as a geographical move. Remember that Scripture is replete with examples of those who took major steps and were fully in God's will in doing so.

Ask God to guide your thinking, and as you prayerfully consider the future, make the best plan you can to improve your circumstances. Commit that plan to the Lord and commit yourself to carrying out that plan. Realize that this step alone is a major beginning, for your subconscious is committed to looking for ways to fulfill the plan. You will now be more alert to opportunities and ready to take advantage of them. Move ahead, and do what needs to be done to accomplish your goal.

Chapter Eleven

Warming Up
to Conversation

A *retired pastor I know made a practice throughout his* ministry of always arriving late to church dinners, parties and social functions. His wife willingly followed along with the routine. The reason was that they felt inept in situations where small talk and informal conversation were required. "We never knew what to say to people on a personal level," he admits.

My guess is that you probably identify with him. Many of us who are shy are uncomfortable initiating conversation with strangers and new acquaintances. It can even be difficult maintaining the flow of conversation with people we know well. Many of us fear unstructured social gatherings such as parties, where there are a number of currents of conversation going on and we are expected to fend for ourselves, with our awkwardness on public display. While we probably feel quite comfortable when someone takes a direct interest in us and draws us out, it's the situations where we're expected to initiate or sustain conversation that we dread.

As with other fears that accompany shyness, let me assure you that the fear of making conversation is *extremely common*. It is experienced by a surprising number of people, including many who seem to be extroverts. Some, like my retired pastor friend, go through a lifetime appearing to be comfortable with people, even achieving success in areas which require some skill in relating to people, yet never feel natural talking with people informally.

Like all shyness fears, the fear of making conversation is self-perpetuating, for it keeps us from the very encounters with people which could sharpen our conversation skills and give us confidence. The good news is that *the skills of conversation can be mastered by anyone*, even the very shy. Because they are so seldom taught during our years of formal education, we often assume they are simply more natural to some than others, and either you have it or you don't. Yet in fact these abilities can be acquired, and this is one of the most encouraging discoveries many of us ever make.

Actually, being a late bloomer in becoming an effective conversationalist has certain advantages. Your quiet nature to this point in life has probably enhanced your ability to listen and allowed your sensitivity to others' feelings to deepen. Thus, you already have one of the most critical social skills, which is empathy. As this is combined with basic skills of interaction, your ability with people can blossom. And the very factors that make you shy will work to your benefit in relating to others.

Indeed, many shy people report that simply learning some conversation skills has improved their social life immensely. Where, then, do we begin?

Visual Communication

We need to begin at the point where conversation itself begins, and that is our body language. Before we convey anything by word of mouth to another person, we communicate volumes through our physical appearance, presence and mannerisms. We simply cannot separate verbal communication from the physical language of communication; the two go hand in hand and work to our benefit or detriment in innumerable ways.

As I'm writing, a woman calls who has been a wheelchair patient all her life, a victim from birth of spina bifida. She is just short of her fiftieth birthday. The call is timely, for I'm reminded that effective body language has little to do with natural attributes of beauty or physical prowess and everything to do with how we *manage* what we have physically—a talent that Judy has mastered quite well. She is highly effective in her communication with others, and that is partly due to the brightness of her demeanor. She has long outlived the life expectancy for spina bifida, and I suspect that too is related to her manner with people, for she has set up a positive cycle of interaction with others which makes her delightful and helps to keep her optimistic. It is not without interest, too, that she has been happily married for fifteen years. Her example gives hope to us all, for it demonstrates that regardless of the deficits we are beginning with physically, we *can* learn competent communication skills, including effective body language.

Yet we tend to downplay the importance of body language as Christians, or we feel squeamish about it as a topic of consideration. "We should be concerned only with the spiritual and not the physical," someone will say. Or, "Others should like me for who I am, in spite of how I come across physically." As we have noted, though, the Bible does not neatly segment the spiritual and physical aspects of human life. *All* of our life is under the lordship of Christ, and each area is important in terms of how God uses us to communicate with others. There is, indeed, a considerable biblical precedent for taking body language seriously; it is found in the fact of the Incarnation. God became *man* in Jesus Christ. He chose to communicate with us not merely in a spiritual fashion but in a physically observable way as well.

Biblical Examples

A considerable respect is shown in Scripture for the role of the physical in communication. Physical features such as countenance, for instance, are often taken as a sign of one's innermost feelings in the interaction which occurs in Scripture. Thus, when Nehemiah became depressed over the fate of Jerusalem, he was not eager to share his feelings with the king. But King Artaxerxes quickly inferred from his demeanor that something was wrong: "Why does your face look so sad when you are not ill? This can be nothing but sadness of heart" (Neh 2:2).

Physical gestures are also an inescapable part of human communication in Scripture. In the Old Testament, bowing was a required sign of respect toward royalty and was practiced in other important human encounters as well. "So Moses went out to meet his father-in-law and bowed down and kissed him" (Ex 18:7). "At this, [Ruth] bowed down with her face to the ground. She exclaimed [to Boaz], 'Why have I found such favor in your eyes that you notice me—a foreigner?' " (Ruth 2:10). "When Mephibosheth son of Jonathan, the son of Saul, came to David, he bowed down to pay him honor" (2 Sam 9:6). In the New Testament Christians are often exhorted to "greet" one another. The literal Greek word for greet is *salute,* and the term is commonly used in the King James and American Standard versions of the Bible. "Salute every saint in Christ Jesus. The brethren which are with me greet you" (Phil 4:21 KJV). The word implies expressing your greeting in a physical manner, through embracing and in some cases kissing. Thus in four of his epistles Paul tells his readers explicitly, "Greet one another with a holy kiss" (Rom 16:16; 1 Cor 16:20; 2 Cor 13:12; 1 Thess 5:26).

Jesus' instruction in the Sermon on the Mount to those who fast is also of interest. "When you fast, do not look somber as the hypocrites do, for they disfigure their faces to show men they are fasting. I tell you the truth, they have received their reward in full. But when you fast, put oil on your head and wash your face, so that it will not be obvious to men that you are fasting" (Mt 6:16-18). While Jesus' primary intent is to exhort believers not to use fasting as a pretext for self-glory, his remarks bring home the fact that God has placed us in a world where the physical communicates. People are conditioned to read our feelings through our body language. I show respect and compassion for others by taking care of my physical appearance and making my best effort to convey positive signals through my physical actions. Obedience to Christ requires that I take the matter of body language seriously.

Scripture also respects the cultural factors in communication (1 Cor 9:19-23), and this is as true for body language as for verbal expression. Gestures and mannerisms which are welcome in one culture may be anathema in another. The biblical examples of body language prod us not to imitate the exact customs but to look seriously at what sort of physical communication works best in the culture where we live.

The Appearance Factor

It starts with our physical appearance. The moment I encounter someone, I make a statement through my appearance. Like it or not, my looks convey a lot of information about how I feel about myself and about that person as well. Caring for my physical appearance is the beginning step in effective communication.

This may not seem to be particularly good news for those of us who are shy, for many shy persons do not feel good about their physical features and not a few regard their shyness as rooted in a poor body image. While lack of esteem for their appearance leads some shy people to excessive concern with diet, grooming and dress, many more are inclined to a what's-the-use attitude and have long given up on making a serious effort to present themselves attractively. Generally, they are as much in need of encouragement as they are of practical pointers on how to improve their appearance.

Fortunately, there is plenty of reason to be encouraged. For one thing, your attractiveness to others depends much more on factors you can control than on those you cannot. If you make a reasonable effort to take care of yourself, to groom appropriately and to dress in a way that enhances your features, others will find you attractive. If the area of grooming and dress is confusing to you, I strongly recommend getting a book on the subject. Carole Jackson's *Color Me Beautiful* (for women) and *Color for Men* are both helpful volumes which give practical advice on how to dress effectively without breaking your budget.[1]

Keep in mind, too, that God has given you your physical features with a very good purpose in mind (Ps 139:15). They are exactly the ones needed for carrying out what he wants you to do and for building relationships which he wants you to develop. You are beginning from a much greater position of strength here than you probably realize. You don't need to become obsessed with making yourself attractive, for God has already given you appropriate features. Simply give some *reasonable* attention to being a good steward of these characteristics. Think of grooming and dress as putting the frame around a picture; the frame should enhance the picture but not overshadow it.

It is encouraging, too, to realize that there is a reciprocal relation between body image and body language. Your physical appearance is part of your body language—but your body language affects how others view your appearance. This is good news, for body language is definitely something we can control. Let's look, then, at how we can make it more effective.

Giving the Right Signals

Within American culture there are certain physical actions which are almost universal in what they communicate. Typically these are not understood or utilized well by shy people. But these points of body language are easily learned and when put into practice can enhance your effectiveness in conversation.

Smile awhile. Though we joke about it and may consider a forced smile to be phony, the fact is that everyone is drawn to a smile in the same way that metal particles are pulled to a magnet. Your smile at someone, whether new acquaintance or old, has the effect of saying to them, "I'm throwing the doors of my life open to you, at least for this moment in time." Smiling periodically during a conversation reinforces your openness, and it is especially appropriate when the other person makes a point which deserves validation. Your smile is one of the most effective means you have for conveying acceptance, affirmation and openness. It does wonders to open the channels of communication. By the same token, the failure to smile will likely be read as rejection or disinterest.

But we who are shy are often uneasy about making a determined effort to smile at someone, for fear our smile will appear insincere or even that our lips will tremble. This is another one of those wonderful points where our shyness can work to our benefit. The fact that you are so concerned about appearing nongenuine provides you a built-in buffer against coming on like a used car salesman from Orange County! I assure you that others will not read your smile as artificial; they will take it as anything but that.

And don't be concerned about quivering lips. We are usually much more aware of trembling in our lips or face than others are. Remember that your lips and facial muscles move anyway when you smile or speak, and others are not likely to notice what additional movement may be there due to nervousness. Even if someone does notice your lips trembling, they will simply take it as part of your humanness. If anything, it will reinforce another's impression that you are being sincere. It will not work against you—indeed, it will work *for* you, as long as you are trying to show an interest in the other person.

I cannot urge you strongly enough to work on your ability to smile at others. If necessary, before going to a social gathering, practice smiling at yourself in the mirror and limber up your facial muscles by stretching your mouth wide open. Make a practice, too, of smiling at individuals you meet in the course of your daily routine—the checkout clerk in the grocery store, the gas station attendant who takes your credit card, the UPS driver who hands you a package. In more significant encounters, make the effort to smile at the person you are meeting or speaking to, even if it seems forced or unnatural to do so. Only through this kind of practice will smiling in conversation become more natural to you. It is a skill, one of the most critical skills of effective communication.

Maintain eye contact. It is also very important to maintain a reasonable level of eye contact with the person you meet or converse with. Shy people often are very uneasy looking at another person directly in the eyes; they tend to look down or away while in conversation. Women generally are more comfortable with eye contact than men, who are more inclined to associate eye-to-eye contact with hostility. In some societies direct eye contact is in fact taken as a sign of contentiousness, and it is occasionally read this way in some sectors of our own society. Yet when direct eye contact is combined with smiling and a warm disposition, most people in American society take it as a sign of friendliness and serious interest in what they have to say. You generally do far better to err on the side of making good eye contact than to shy away from it.

This doesn't mean that you need to stare continuously into another's eyes while speaking. Staring away for a brief moment or focusing your gaze on another portion of the person's face for a time is fine. But make the effort to stay eye-to-eye for the majority of time in the conversation. Eye contact is particularly important when you first meet or greet people or try to get their attention in a crowd.

If eye contact is painful or unnatural for you, I urge you to work at it. Practice it constantly in less threatening situations, such as paying the grocery clerk or talking with someone you know well. In higher-risk situations, such as talking with someone you would like to date, make an extra effort to look into the eyes of that person. However unnatural this practice may feel to you, it will work much more to your benefit in conversation than staring away. And with practice this response will become much more natural. Good eye contact is indispensable to good communication.

Shake a hand if you can. Okay, I'm from Washington, D.C., but even if I weren't, I would still insist that a warm handshake is one of the most effective means to break the ice in meeting or greeting someone. I'm convinced that the handshake in our culture today is the closest parallel we have to the New Testament practice of the salute. Unlike a hug or embrace, which may be interpreted as too forward, the handshake is universally accepted in our society as an appropriate and cordial greeting. And it has evolved from being primarily a routine among males to being a fitting greeting between women, and between men and women, as well.

The handshake is also a virtually guaranteed *safe* form of salute. By that I mean it almost always assures a reciprocal response from the other. While I can think of several occasions when I reached out my arms to hug someone I was greeting and was embarrassed by not being hugged back, I cannot remember a single time of extending my hand to shake another's when the handshake was not returned. Handshaking is so instinctive in our culture that you may rest assured you will not be humiliated if you make the first move.

In taking this initiative, you will gain the greatest advantage in most social encounters. When you approach someone to speak with him or her, be the first to thrust your hand forward for a handshake. When this effort is combined with a warm smile and, yes, eye contact, you will almost certainly get a positive response. Of course, if someone beats you to the punch in initiating a handshake, be flattered and not offended. But don't assume that another will take this initiative; after all, the other person may be shyer than you are. Be the first to put out your hand, and take encouragement that you have this simple and almost magical tool for initiating conversation. Take full advantage of it (and if you must, take some inspiration from Washington!).

To hug or not to hug? In many Christian circles friendly hugging is common as a form of greeting or saying goodby between members of the same or opposite sex. Customs vary from group to group, however, and I can only say observe how others respond, and when in Rome . . .

Of course, if someone reaches out to hug you, respond; don't leave that person feeling sheepish for making the effort. And if you are in a group which is comfortable with hugging, always err on the side of keeping a hug brief and simple. Never hug another in way that might cause that person to feel exploited (as a shy person you are probably not in danger of doing this anyway). A brief side hug around the shoulders or waist is usually the safest bet.

If you do have the mortifying experience of extending your arms to hug someone and get no response, don't die. Some people (usually ones who are quite shy themselves) simply have not become comfortable with hugging, and it is probably not a rejection of you personally. You will find that most people will respond positively, so chalk this one up to experience and move on.

Consider your stance. Finally, there are a variety of gestures and mannerisms which work for us or against us in social encounters. Often these are automatic responses which we may not even be conscious of displaying. Yet they quickly, if unwittingly, convey warmth or coldness to another person. As shy persons we need to be particularly conscious of these mannerisms, for our nervousness with people may make us inclined to body language which implies boredom or irritation with them—even when this is the last thing we want to convey. But with practice these patterns can be changed to more congenial signals.

As I've been writing this section, I've been walking around the room with my arms folded—a stance which I find very comfortable when thinking. Yet I have to be careful not to do this in conversation, for crossed arms are often read by another as a sign of skepticism or annoyance. Nervousness may incline us to fold our arms when we're talking with someone or sitting by ourselves at a social gathering. But that gives a message to others to keep their distance. We need to be watchful of that tendency and make the effort to avoid it in public. Generally we convey greater warmth by letting our arms hang at our sides and then raising our hands slightly (but not demonstratively) when speaking or making an important point.

We should also be careful not to clench our fists, for that can make others feel uneasy or intimidated. If nervousness inclines you to want to do this, consciously resist the tendency and let your hands hang limp. You will not only improve your effectiveness in conversation but counteract a physical mechanism which increases your anxiety.

Common habits such as pulling at the nose or chin, twitching a mustache or stroking the hair, while acceptable if only occasional, become annoying if carried on continually. Any of these habits can be avoided with some effort; the benefits to good conversation make the effort well worthwhile.

On the positive side, it is a good idea to tilt your head slightly and to nod occasionally while in conversation. These gestures convey an openness and interest in what the other has to say. Make a point of standing fairly close—but not obnoxiously close—to the person you are talking with. A two-foot distance is a good rule of thumb, in our culture.

I would encourage you to make a practice of observing the physical responses others display in conversation. Make a mental note of which ones help you feel comfortable and which ones tend to alienate you. Then work at adopting those responses which you feel work best. In this area as in all others, the best rule of thumb is to do unto others as you would have them do unto you.

Chapter Twelve

Knowing What to Say

While we who are shy usually benefit from learning more effective body language, we often need to work on our verbal communication skills as well. Confronting this area can seem especially intimidating, for this is precisely where shyness is rooted for many of us. *The fear that we cannot function effectively in conversation—particularly with strangers and new acquaintances—is our greatest insecurity.* We may be convinced that we lack the potential ever to become an effective conversationalist.

But my personal experience and the testimony of many shy people convince me that each of us can improve substantially in our verbal communication skills if we simply make a reasonable effort. The principles of effective conversation are not hard to understand and put into practice. And we who are shy have certain advantages in conversation which become evident as we become more active conversationalists.

Recently I received a letter from a friend, who mentioned that her husband is teaching their son how to carry on conversation.

He uses a helpful analogy to explain the dynamics of conversation. She writes, "Greg has always been a wonderful conversationalist. Now he's trying to teach our eleven-year-old Matt that conversation is like playing catch. The ball is thrown to you; you hold it for a moment and toss it back. Ideally, neither person holds the ball too long."

I like this analogy because it speaks of the *momentum* which takes place in conversation. What we who are shy most fear about the conversation process is that it all depends upon us. We imagine that this enormous weight of responsibility to keep the conversation going will suddenly be upon our shoulders, as though we were called to give a long monologue to a demanding audience. In fact, the other person carries at least as much responsibility in the conversation process and can take even more of it if we allow them to. On top of this is the wonderful fact of momentum. As the conversation continues, a natural flow takes over; we are drawn into the process and forget our anxiety. The conversation indeed has an energy of its own, and the comparison to the game of catch is quite accurate. You don't have to be a star pitcher; the secret is simply to keep the ball in motion. Here are some tips which can help in doing that.

1. Introduce yourself. When you see someone at a social event whom you want to meet, walk up to that person, extend your hand and introduce yourself. Likewise, when you meet someone for the first time and that person does not take the initiative to tell you his or her name, quickly put forth your hand and give your name. As simple as this point would seem to be, many shy people do not take the initiative to introduce themselves. Even if they become engrossed in conversation with a new acquaintance at a party, they may let the conversation come and go without ever giving their name. They fear that introducing themselves is too forward, that the other will not be interested in knowing who they are, or even that they might be rebuffed for taking this step.

Giving someone your name, though, almost always has the effect of putting that person at ease. It's a gesture of openness and trust, a very safe step and one that is virtually guaranteed to put you in a position of strength at the beginning of a conversation. Most of the time, the person will immediately respond by giving you his or her name in return; the ball quickly bounces back. If this doesn't happen, you don't have reason to be offended; in fact you can take encouragement in knowing this probably means the other person is even shyer than you are. It is quite appropriate in this case to *ask* the other person their name—even to do so in a lighthearted way. With a grin, ask, "What do they call *you?*" I assure you that other people will be relieved and flattered that you ask and delighted for the chance to identify themselves. Yet in most cases you will not need to go this far. Simply introducing yourself will evoke the reciprocal reaction.

2. Don't be afraid of small talk. Many shy people feel queasy about small talk, for fear the other person will be bored or think it is stupid. They fear that beginning a conversation with a remark about the weather or a comment about incidental details in the setting where they are meeting seems superficial; it implies to the other that they are lacking in personal depth. Yet in reality, small talk is universally employed among people of all educational and economic levels as a means of breaking the ice in conversation.

I would go so far as to say that small talk is a God-ordained means of putting another person at ease and showing the love of Christ to someone in the early stages of a conversation. It was apparently an accepted part of the salute, or greeting, in the New Testament era. One of the reasons Jesus gave his disciples the otherwise puzzling command "do not greet anyone on the road" (Lk 10:4) is that so much small talk was involved in the elaborate greetings of the time that he did not want his disciples diverted from the task at hand—which was to get to the next town and evangelize. But under normal conditions of meeting people and preparing to share the gospel with them, small talk was apparently an important part of the warming-up process in New Testament times.

When you begin a conversation with a new acquaintance or someone you already know, look for incidental details about which you can comment. If you can pay this person a compliment for something he is wearing or something she has accomplished, that is a wonderful way to begin. Or remark about details in the setting where you are meeting. If you are attending a party in someone's home, there is probably something in the room which interests you—a painting, a piece of antique furniture, a coffee-table book. Point out that you find this item interesting and ask the other what he or she thinks. You will probably be surprised to find how quickly the ball begins bouncing with simple comments like these. You will soon establish the beginning of a casual relationship, simply by exchanging smiles and comments on something you have in common (even if it's only the weather or the food).

And yes, it is quite appropriate to comment on the weather. Don't fear you are being uncreative in doing so. In the Washington area where I live the weather is a topic of endless interest, and with good reason: it changes constantly, and the forecasters are wrong more often than not in their predictions. Just this week their emphatic predictions of a major snowstorm again proved inaccurate. No one knows that better than my boys, who stayed up late the night before convinced school would be canceled, only to find themselves somberly walking to the bus in the rain the next morning. This one bad call by the forecasters has provided plenty of fuel for conversation among people in my area.

3. Put the emphasis upon asking questions. The most common mistake people make in conversation is not talking too little but talking too much. Assertive people are sometimes very poor conversationalists, for they spend too much energy focusing upon themselves and too little showing interest in the other person. They bowl someone over with tales of their own experience, while all the while the other is longing for a chance to share. This is where the shy person has a considerable advantage in conversation. You are already comfortable being quiet and letting another person talk. The good news is that this is often the very best way to behave in conversation, as long as you take the right steps to trigger some response from the other. The secret to doing this simply lies in asking the right questions.

Ritual questions which will probably bring a brief response are a good place to start. "Is this your first time visiting this church?" "Are you a native of this area?" "Where do you hail from?" "Where do you work?"

But carefully think through questions which require a more elaborate and thoughtful response, which will spur the other to share more details about their life. "What was it like growing up on a farm in Kansas?" "What do you see as the greatest challenge facing the industry with which you work?" "What do you think the outcome of our church's building drive will be?"

As a conversation evolves, it is particularly good to ask questions which prod another to share not just facts and opinions but *feelings*. "Was it lonely living in a remote rural town?" "Did you find it frightening to grow up in New York City?" "What do you find most enjoyable about your current job?" "What do you like best about the church you attend?" "Do you find parenting a preschooler overwhelming?" A person's responses to questions like these will give you some treasured insight into his or her human side. They will be grateful, too, that you are showing this level of interest in them.

4. Listen carefully for pertinent information. As a person shares, be alert for three types of details:

☐ *Free information.* People will likely go down many rabbit trails as they talk with you. Even a brief answer to a question will probably provide you with additional details about this individual beyond what you have asked. This "free information" is a treasure trove of data for further questions or comments. To the question, "How long have you lived in Cincinnati?" for instance, someone might respond, "I moved here from Kansas City three years ago to take a job with Procter and Gamble." In that one sentence she has told you not only how long she has resided in the city but (a) whom she works for; (b) the fact that she previously did *not* work for this company; (c) the city that she hailed from previously. The answer also tells you that she has made a *major* move, a fact that may reveal an important window on her character.

With this free information you have a number of possible jumping-off points for further questions: "Tell me about your work with P & G—are you in sales or research?" "Do you like Cincinnati better than KC?" "Did you grow up in Kansas?" "Was it hard making the move?" "Whom did you work for before moving here?" "Is our bleak weather easier to take than Kansas humidity?"

☐ *Iceberg statements.* Don Gabor refers to this type of comment in *How to Start a Conversation and Make Friends,* and I find the distinction helpful.[1] Often in conversation someone will make a brief remark which suggests that a lot of emotion or personal experience underlies the statement. The comment is merely the tip of the iceberg of some deep-seated feelings and concerns— an invaluable piece of free information. Suppose, for instance, that your new friend from Procter and Gamble remarks that the company has placed her in a sales position in spite of the fact that she would much rather be in research. This tells you that she is probably frustrated with her work, feels she is missing her niche, may be more of an introvert than an extrovert, and likely feels she is not being treated justly by her employer. You again have many jumping-off points for further discussion.

An appropriate response at this point might be, "They must

see you as multigifted. Do you think they understand you would
rather be in research?" Or, "What is it about research that you
like better than sales?"

☐ *Points of identity.* As someone speaks with you, you will likely
find many surprising areas of identity with this person—points
where your interests or experiences connect. You remember, for
instance, that in high school you spent a sweltering week in
August with your parents in Kansas City while your dad was on a
business trip. The temperature was in the high nineties the
entire week, with equal humidity. You have an experience to
share with your new friend and a basis to ask her if this is typical
of Kansas weather in the summer. On a more serious level, she
may mention that she attended a Baptist church in KC but has
not found one she is comfortable with in Cincinnati. You are
familiar with several and can tell her what you know—perhaps
even invite her to attend a service at one with you.

5. Jump in where appropriate. As long as the other person seems
comfortable sharing, and as long as you are comfortable listening, don't feel anxious about needing to stoke the conversation.
Your strength is in listening; use that strength to full advantage.
Do add some occasional interjections like "That's really interesting" or "I appreciate your sharing this," and by all means let your
facial expressions indicate that you are interested in what this
person is saying. But allow the person the leisure to share as
much or as little as he or she wishes (remembering that lots of
people are shy!), and don't feel trigger-happy about having to
jump in. When a pause occurs, then go ahead with a further
question or comment. If you have discovered a point of identity
with this person, share it; the point of identity does not have to
be profound but can be any area of experience that might relate
to this person's life or be interesting to him or her.

In talking with your new friend from Kansas, for instance, you
could say something about your experience growing up in Cincinnati. She probably still thinks of herself as an outsider to some

extent and enjoys hearing the perspective of long-time residents.

Two points of advice, however. Don't feel that you have to wait for another person to ask you a question about yourself before it is appropriate to share something about your experience. My experience is that most new acquaintances are not inclined to ask personal questions of you at early points in a conversation, simply because they are feeling awkward themselves and are more concerned with coming up with something interesting to say to you. Some folks never ask a question during an entire conversation. If that makes you feel they dislike you, disregard your feeling. Most people—to put it simply—have never had any training in how to carry on a congenial conversation, and the thought of asking a personal question simply does not occur to them. The fact is, by digesting and putting into practice the little bit of advice which is in this chapter, you will have more skill in conversation than a lot of the people with whom you converse. Take encouragement from that.

But remember that even when people do not ask you a direct question about yourself, they will probably appreciate your sharing some details about your life—especially if you have already made the effort to take an interest in them. This allows them a chance to breathe and to gather their own thoughts.

Be careful not to inundate someone else with what you have to say, especially if he or she is a new acquaintance. This might seem like an unnecessary caution. You may fear talking without interruption to a stranger for more than ten seconds! It frequently happens, though, that as shy persons become more comfortable with conversation, they get carried away in their sharing, as though to overcompensate for their tendency to be silent. Unless you have reason to know that your new acquaintance is keenly interested in what you are sharing, don't talk for more than two or three minutes without making the effort to draw him back into the conversation. Remember that, however interested he may be in what you are saying, he probably desires even more to share his own experience with you. Allow him fair opportunity to do that—even err on that side when talking with a new friend. Keep the ball-tossing analogy in mind.

6. *Don't be afraid of appearing uninformed.* A major reason why we who are shy hesitate to ask questions of others—especially relating to their work or personal interests—is our fear of appearing ignorant. We assume others think we should be knowledgeable about their field of experience, and we do not want to be judged unenlightened. I may hesitate to ask someone to describe his work with computers, for instance, for fear of revealing that I don't know the difference between a floppy disk and a monitor.

Keep in mind, though, that we live in an age of specialization where, by definition, each person's knowledge—no matter how extensive—can only be a small fraction of the total pool of human wisdom. Most people appreciate this and are not expecting you necessarily to share their areas of knowledge or competence. Indeed, an informed person recognizes that Renaissance men and women simply do not exist in today's climate of specialization. Realize that the other person will probably be flattered by your question and affirmed to know that his or her area of expertise is something you are interested in learning more about. It is highly unlikely that he or she will judge you ignorant—but if so, this is not the kind of person you want to bother getting to know anyway. Err on the side of being inquisitive. Nothing ventured, nothing gained! (A tip: Say "I don't know much about . . ." as you ask your question, if you wish, but don't say "This question of mine is really stupid." There is no need to indict yourself unnecessarily, and no sincere question is a stupid one.)

7. *Be affirming.* Another point that can scarcely be emphasized strongly enough is our need to affirm, compliment and encourage those whom we speak with in friendly conversation. Herein lies one of the most critical secrets of strong and lasting friend-

ships. When you look carefully at such relationships, you usually find that a great deal of mutual affirmation and encouragement is constantly going on. We usually underestimate another's need for affirmation. We may imagine that someone who is successful, is in leadership, or seems comfortable socially does not need to be affirmed. Usually nothing could be further from the truth. Charlie Shedd is right when he compares our need for affirmation to a tire with a slow leak: You pump it up at night and the next day it needs to be pumped up again.

Some believers make the mistaken assumption that Christians should be above the need for human affirmation or encouragement—they should learn to receive their praise from Christ alone, in other words. In reality, Scripture puts considerable emphasis upon the importance of our being *channels* of God's encouragement by taking the initiative to affirm each other. "Outdo one another in showing honor" to each other, Paul declares in Romans 12:10 (RSV). It is the only command in Scripture where we are challenged to try to *outdo* each other at something!

We who are shy are too often hesitant with our praise, and others may conclude that we are snobbish because of our failure to compliment. If giving affirmation is difficult for you, work at it and work at it hard. Look for small ways to compliment the person you are speaking with, simply as part of casual conversation. Let people know that you like what they are wearing or appreciate something they have to say. I urge you to push yourself to do this even if you feel squeamish. It is a vital step forward in your ability to interact comfortably with others in conversation. Think of how you would like someone to compliment you, and then affirm that person in the same way. Don't wait for the other to do it first.

8. Share your opinions. This doesn't mean you shouldn't express your opinions or "beg to differ" with someone if you see matters differently. Indeed, others will more likely be drawn to you if they know you have convictions and are willing to stand up for them than if you always just nod in agreement. But there is an art to sharing a difference of opinion, especially in friendly conversation. Express it in a way that is both affirming and humble. Before doing so, tell the other person that you appreciate and respect his or her viewpoint. You are open, too, to hearing more about why he or she feels this way. But here's how you see it at this time. You realize you may not have all the facts, but this is how it seems to you.

Good friendship can survive and even prosper when differences of viewpoint are shared in such an atmosphere of acceptance and humility.

At all costs, avoid being argumentative. Avoid being drawn into the compulsion to prove yourself right. Don't feel that every nook and cranny of an issue has to be explored, either; this is merely one conversation. Save something for Act II and Act III!

9. Remember names! Make every effort to remember the name of the person you are speaking with, after hearing it only once. Don't let the thought that you are not good at remembering names discourage you from trying. A name is only a few syllables long, at most, and is not a vast store of information to retain. Any of us can remember another's name with a little effort. Associate it quickly in your mind with some detail about the person, however absurd, and continue to roll that name over in your mind in the early minutes of speaking with the person. *Use* the name as often as possible, short of being overbearing, in talking with your new acquaintance. "You know, Patty, that's a really interesting point." There are few sounds in life we enjoy hearing more than our own name spoken by someone else. The simple practice of interjecting someone's name into the conversation will go a long way toward helping the person feel comfortable and affirmed—*and* toward helping you retain the name for future use.

If another person whom you know comes along while you're conversing with someone, quickly introduce these two people by name to each other. Unless you know for sure, don't assume they have already been introduced; err on the side of assuming they have not been, even if you might have seen them talking before. Many people converse at a party or gathering without bothering to introduce themselves. You'll do them both a favor by taking this initiative and will gain favor in both of their eyes by doing it as well. When unsure, you can simply say, "Walter, have you met Carlos?" If they say yes, no problem. If no, go on to tell each the other's name and one thing about him or her.

If you do forget someone's name, ask again. Forgetting a name is not the unpardonable sin, and most people realize that most others are not good at remembering names. The fact that you are concerned enough to inquire again will speak well for you and be affirming to the person with whom you are talking. You can excuse yourself by saying something like, "Forgive me, but this has been a long day and my brain is on overload. Could you please give me your name again?" You may find that they have forgotten yours as well and are grateful for this excuse to ask *you* again. Or you can offer it, just as a reminder.

10. Hold on to details after the conversation. After a conversation is over, make a conscientious effort to remember information, including names and small details, which a person shares with you, especially if this is someone you expect to run into or wish to encounter again. When you get home, record the information in a journal or on a file card. Be a good steward with the information about this person's life which God has entrusted to you through the conversation. Remember it. If you consider it significant, pray about it on the person's behalf. And review it when you expect to see the person again. You will be exercising an important aspect of Christ's love by doing this. And you will greatly enhance your potential for continued friendship with this person.

I personally keep separate files in my cabinet on dozens of friends and acquaintances. No, I'm not playing Ross Perot or CIA in doing this. I'm simply making a point of holding on to pertinent details about their lives to aid my feeble brain when the time comes to write them or talk with them. Into the file goes a birth announcement (remembering the names of children of distant acquaintances is especially hard), a note or form letter (common at Christmas) which I receive from them, or a note which I make about information they share with me. The practice has helped me considerably, especially in maintaining friendships with people I see only occasionally.

Find what practice will best help you remember the details others share with you, and follow it diligently.

Moving Forward

In this section we've considered steps to take as shy individuals to enhance our social life. I've offered advice for putting yourself in the best situations for meeting people, as well as suggestions for improving your conversation skills. I've focused on the area where our inhibitions are usually greatest as shy persons, which is taking the first steps to meet people and build relationships.

In the remaining chapters I will offer advice on becoming more assertive, gaining an optimistic outlook and handling public-speaking situations. All of these areas relate in important ways to improving our social life. There is certainly more that can be said about building friendships and relationships. Much of it, though, goes beyond the scope of a single book. My book *Should I Get Married?* considers practical steps that can be taken to find a serious relationship which may lead to marriage, as well as how to judge your compatibility with someone else. You may find it helpful as a companion volume to this book.[2]

Helpful books on the subjects of dating and building friendship include Em Griffin's *Making Friends (& Making Them Count)*[3] and Joyce Huggett's *Dating, Sex and Friendship*.[4] I also recommend Don Gabor's *How to Start a Conversation and Make Friends* (mentioned earlier), if you would like more advice on developing conversational skills.

Part Four

Asserting Yourself— and Your Life

Chapter Thirteen

Faith and Assertiveness

It is 10:30 Saturday evening when Susan's phone rings. Tired and wanting to ignore it, she lets it continue to the fourth ring, then out of guilt picks it up.

"Hi, how are you? This is Pat," a woman's voice announces. Before Susan can respond, Pat continues, "Hon, I know this is asking a lot, but could you pick me up at the bus station and drive me home? I've just gotten back from San Diego."

"Do you have the money to take a taxi?" Susan asks.

"If I have to," Pat responds. "But you know, Christmas is only a month away, and I really need to conserve . . ."

Susan, already worn out, still has work to do on her junior-high lesson for Sunday morning. The bus station is twenty minutes away and Pat's home is on the other side of town. By the time she'd get back, there would be no energy left for her Sunday-school preparation. Besides, Pat has taken advantage of her more times than Susan can remember.

Susan would like to tell Pat that she has neither the time nor the energy to come for her. And, when she can collect herself, she would like to speak honestly with Pat about her presumptuousness. Yet Susan remembers Jesus' admonition to go the second mile. "Isn't this a clear situation where I need to bend for someone else?" she wonders. "And wouldn't confronting Pat be a violation of Jesus' command to turn the other cheek? Doesn't God require me to deny myself for the sake of Pat's needs?"

The Ongoing Question
To assert yourself, or not to? To stand up for yourself, or to go along with someone else's wishes or designs for you? We struggle with this issue often as Christians. For Susan, the question is whether to cave in to a friend's unreasonable expectations. Like her, we each face situations where people try to take advantage of us, including times when friends expect too much of us and intimidating instances when someone in business tries to exploit us. For the sensitive Christian, the question arises, "Should I stand up for my rights—or is it better to give in?"

Of course, in some situations the concern is not with standing up for our rights but simply with whether to express ourselves straightforwardly. Should I speak up and say what I'm thinking in this class? Should I tell her how much I care for her? Should I share my faith with him? Should I be overt in stating my qualifications in this job interview? And in a broader sense we always face the assertiveness question in considering major steps of faith: Should I take initiative to find a better job or simply wait for the Lord to provide it? Should I take determined initiative to find someone to marry or merely stay passive in the matter?

Healthy Assertiveness
Shy people are uncomfortable asserting ourselves in some situations, and many of us are uneasy being assertive in *any* setting. One major problem is our fear of people. We fear we will not be successful in our attempts to be assertive and will experience

unbearable embarrassment in the process. Learning how to confront and manage our fears is a major step forward in becoming more assertive. In general, too, we need a more optimistic outlook about our possibilities for success.

Often we are hindered by misconceptions about biblical teaching on assertiveness. We are uneasy with the concept of assertiveness for Christians, for we fear it implies behavior that is patently un-Christian. Being assertive, we assume, means always demanding our rights, trampling over the needs of others and feeling the freedom to blow our lid whenever we feel like it. That's not being assertive; that's being obnoxious! Such behavior is contrary to the teaching and example of Christ.

Most writers and teachers who promote assertiveness have two general goals in mind. One is to help individuals "own" their own lives—to break free of the control of others' expectations and be in control of their emotions when they speak. If I vent anger at others, for instance, it suggests not that I am being freely assertive but that I am letting their expectations control me, for I have allowed them to upset me. Owning my own life will more likely be reflected in my responding calmly, even politely, to them. Thus the feisty Manuel J. Smith, author of a bestselling book on assertiveness, *When I Say No I Feel Guilty,* devotes a surprising portion of his book to helping readers learn to accept criticism graciously and nondefensively.[1]

The other aim of assertiveness training is to encourage individuals to take the initiative (1) to carry out what they feel is best to do with their lives and (2) to express their convictions and concerns clearly and honestly to others. This self-expression is not to be done at the wholesale expense of others' feelings; indeed, assertiveness is most effective when exercised with empathy and compassion. Still, expressing yourself is important. It contributes not only to your own well-being and fruitfulness but to the quality of your friendships and relationships as well.

When defined in this way, the idea of being assertive is not incompatible with Paul's instruction in Ephesians 4:15 that we are to speak the truth in love to each other. Indeed, that verse gives a clear admonition to Christians to be assertive, at least within certain boundaries. Still, as shy Christians we are more likely to think of the boundaries than of the freedom or mandate implied in any biblical notion of assertiveness. And the idea that we should own our own life seems to fly in the face of what we have long been taught. Constantly we have heard that we must sacrifice our interests for the needs of others and lay down our lives for their sake. Can such unselfishness possibly reconcile with owning our lives?

Owning Your Own Life

In fact it can, and the two concepts go hand in hand in Scripture. In the biblical understanding, I am called to give myself to another's needs not because I cannot do otherwise but because I decide to do so *as a free choice.* It is this aspect of my decision to help another that makes it a true response of Christian compassion. Yet I can only give myself freely to another if I own my life in the first place. It is in this spirit that Paul declares, "Though I am free and belong to no man, I make myself a slave to everyone, to win as many as possible" (1 Cor 9:19). Here and elsewhere Paul seems to give about equal emphasis to the cherished freedom he experiences as a child of Christ and the free choice he makes to invest his life for the sake of others. Because he is free to begin with, he is able to make this choice in a genuinely compassionate and not codependent fashion.

When we look for it, in fact, we find this assumption implicit whenever the Scriptures urge us to give ourselves to the needs of others: we must first own our own lives. It is there, for instance, in various descriptions of Jesus himself. He was able to wash his disciples' feet because of the strong sense of identity he had in the first place: "Jesus, knowing that the Father had given all things into his hands, and that he had come from God and was going to God, rose from supper, laid aside his garments, and girded himself with a towel. Then he poured water into a basin, and began to wash the disciples' feet" (Jn 13:4-5 RSV).

It is there, too, in the place where we would least expect to find it—Jesus' teaching in the Sermon on the Mount on turning the other cheek. In Matthew 5:38-42 Jesus cautions against a retributive spirit and outlines three situations where one should give double compliance to an aggressor:

"You have heard that it was said, 'Eye for eye, and tooth for tooth.' But I tell you, Do not resist an evil person. If someone strikes you on the right cheek, turn to him the other also. And if someone wants to sue you and take your tunic, let him have your cloak as well. If someone forces you to go one mile, go with him two miles. Give to the one who asks you, and do not turn away from the one who wants to borrow from you."

At first it might seem that Jesus is exhorting us to be a doormat for the aggression and abuse of others, and many Christians have taken his teaching in exactly that way. I believe this is the last thing Jesus meant to imply. Rather, by urging double compliance he was telling us to *take control* of an unjust situation.

By choosing to walk a second mile with someone instead of the single mile he insists upon, I demonstrate that I am deciding for myself what my response to his demand will be. From this angle, going the second mile or turning the other cheek is a profoundly assertive act. In addition, this double compliance aims at having a redemptive effect on the other person, in at least two ways: it shows him I will not let him manipulate me and perhaps removes his desire to do so; it also shames him for his decision to take advantage of me.

Considering the Outcome

This understanding is truly liberating, for it suggests that if turning the other cheek will not affect another person redemptively, or if it would result in harm to someone else, I am not expected to respond in this way. The Mennonite men who, because they believed passivity was required by Christ's admonition to turn the other cheek, stood by and let soldiers rape their wives during the Russian revolution seriously misunderstood Jesus' intent. There are also numerous situations of personal injustice where I am not helping anyone by complying with the injury or by rolling over and playing dead. A woman married to an abusive husband will not be helping him or herself by allowing him to malign or beat her.

In the same way, I am usually kidding myself if I think there is any positive Christian witness involved in allowing someone in a modern business situation to take advantage of me financially. There is an impersonal climate in most business transactions in which turning the other cheek is not effective.

If a car dealership performs shoddy repairs on my car, for instance, individuals there will not be the least bit helped in their spiritual journey if I decide not to complain. They will not likely have any inkling of my spiritual convictions or connect my action with turning the other cheek. The proper Christian action in this case will be to point out the problem to them and calmly but persistently insist that the proper repair be made, for by doing so I will be denting their conviction that they can take advantage of their customers.

Does the Shoe Fit?

I also doubt that Jesus meant to lay the requirement of turning the other cheek upon all believers at all stages in their spiritual development. The instruction was given to his "disciples" (Mt 5:1), perhaps indicating those who were at a stage of growth where they were ready to handle this level of response to people. Of particular interest is that among the multitude of instances in the Gospels where Jesus healed someone who was physically or emotionally ill, there is not one case where he preached self-denial or the need for noble sacrifice to that person. Instead, and without exception, he healed the one who was sick and did not immediately lay the burden of moving mountains upon him or her. When a man whom Jesus healed asked if he could travel with him, Jesus told him instead to return to his home, undoubtedly because Jesus knew the man was not yet ready for such heroics (Mk 5:18-20). It was those who were well, those had a healthy sense of self-identity, that Jesus urged to self-denial. They were able to give themselves to others for his sake because they had a self to give.

There is, in short, a developmental process in becoming assertive which is fully in accord with biblical teaching. Turning the other cheek is an ideal to strive for, but we must be honest with ourselves as to whether we are at a point where we can do it in a way that is mature, honest and healthy. As a shy person, you have probably found it difficult to stand up for yourself, to express yourself freely with others and to make choices for your life which are free from the tyranny of others' expectations. Allow yourself a period to grow and to come more fully into the experience of owning your own life. Then, when you can truly do it as a free choice, be open to those special situations where Christ may call you to turn the other cheek. For now, focus upon learning to be more assertive and realize that by doing so you are taking responsible stewardship for your life as a Christian.

There is one other point to keep in mind in turning-the-other-cheek situations. As my friend Dr. Omar Omland points out in his inspiring book *The Third Mile,* while Jesus spoke of double compliance in certain situations, he did not speak of *triple* compliance.[2] While he encouraged the second mile, in other words, he did not necessarily recommend a third mile. Even in those situations where it may be redemptive to go the second mile, there is a limit to how fully we may be expected to comply. In all cases, the critical need is that our responses to the needs of others are *free* responses. We are called first to own our own lives and then to respond to others' needs in light of the energy God gives us and the particular priorities he lays upon us.

Chapter Fourteen

Taking Initiative

We are called to be assertive as Christians. In our relationships with individuals, this means we are not to be doormats. To the contrary, we are urged by Scripture to make free choices in responding to their expectations in light of what we best understand God wants us to do.

But what about the broader question of asserting our life? Throughout this book I've suggested that there are many times when Christ expects us to take initiative—even bold initiative—to find the best opportunities for building relationships and realizing our potential. Yet how does this reconcile with the biblical emphasis upon living by faith and trusting in Christ to provide? It will help to give some closer attention to this critical question now.

Prudence or Presumption?
Frankly, there are few questions which confuse us more as Christians than what it means to live by faith. When does it mean

sitting still and leaving a need completely in the hands of Christ? When does it mean taking initiative to solve a problem or reach a goal?

Many serious Christians assume that faith usually means the former and not the latter. Jack longs for a new job which would make better use of his gifts. Yet he fears he would be pushing God by going out and looking for one. "Shouldn't I assume that if Christ wants me in a different job, he will bring it along without any effort on my part?" he asks.

Mary Alice, a woman who wants to be married, wrestles with a similar question. She would like to change jobs or even move to a different city where the prospects of meeting someone compatible would be better. Yet she wonders if this would be taking matters too much into her own hands. Doesn't faith demand that she do nothing and wait for Christ to bring the right man directly to her?

Both Jack and Mary Alice would prefer to be doing something specific toward reaching their goals, and they each see clear steps they could take. They both feel frustrated and helpless in the face of dilemmas they feel they could do something to remedy. Yet they fear their efforts would usurp God's authority. Surely faith must require they sit still and wait for him to act.

I remember well carrying this assumption as a young believer, yet I remember too the day when my thinking began to change. I had been considering the possibility of beginning a radio ministry, which seemed a logical outgrowth of my experiences and contacts at the time. Yet I felt painfully guilty about doing anything direct to bring this about. I had heard so much talk about being still and waiting on the Lord that it seemed inconceivable he would want me to take any initiative toward this desire.

Finally I asked an older Christian whom I greatly respected for her counsel. I really expected her to tell me to be passive and wait for the Lord to open any doors. To my surprise, she not only affirmed my dream but recommended I take some determined steps to follow it. Because I thought highly of her and knew she trusted strongly in Christ, I was left feeling much better about the matter of taking personal initiative. Though the radio ministry never got off the ground, her advice helped give me the strength of heart to pursue a music ministry and some other projects in my early years as a believer.

Over the years, though, I've continued to wrestle with the connection between being passive and being active in the Christian life. When does faith require the one and when the other? It finally occurred to me several years ago that the relation between these two in Scripture is really much more straightforward and easy to understand than I had thought. Here is a way of explaining it that I am finding increasingly helpful.

Resting in Faith vs. Steps of Faith

To begin with, there are really two different levels of faith which we are called to at various times as believers. At one level, we are to be inactive and wait patiently for the Lord to move. Here faith involves believing that Christ will bring a solution apart from any work on our end. It is shown in so many situations in Scripture where people were either told to be still or forced to sit and wait for the Lord to act. Examples include Joseph in prison, the Israelites in front of the impassable Jordan River, and the disciples of Jesus who before his ascension were instructed, "Do not leave Jerusalem, but wait for the gift my Father promised" (Acts 1:4).

Yet Scripture just as frequently affirms the faith involved in taking personal responsibility. There are so many impressive pictures in Scripture of individuals who without any divine revelation or special prompting took bold steps to reach a personal goal: Naomi and Ruth moving from Moab to Bethlehem, Nehemiah courageously organizing the Israelites to rebuild Jerusalem, Paul knocking on many doors to find opportunities to preach—in his own words, "making it my ambition to preach the gospel" (Rom 15:20 RSV).

Just as much faith is needed, in fact, for taking personal initiative as for waiting passively for the Lord to provide. While Ruth, for instance, would have been commended for staying in Moab and waiting for God to heal the heartbreak of her husband's death, she probably showed greater faith in going to Bethlehem. By moving forward she placed herself in a vulnerable position where, with Naomi, she would trust the Lord to protect her, to open doors and to make her venture successful. It is interesting that this very move opened her to the relationship with Boaz, who became her husband.

It is right, then, to speak of a second level of faith which we are called to exercise as Christians. At this level we are active and assertive. We take initiative to find the answer to a need. And by moving forward we force ourselves to a dependence on the Lord which would not be possible if we merely sat still.

But when does God want us to operate at level one and when at level two? Let me suggest a rule of thumb which I think applies in most cases: If we are facing a seemingly insurmountable problem—a situation which we perceive we are powerless to influence—we should stay at level-one faith. If there is a reasonable step we can take to improve things or to move toward a goal, then we should assume God wants us to operate at level-two faith. This only makes sense in that, as we function at level-two faith, there is always plenty of opportunity for level-one faith as well. That is, as we move forward there are always unexpected obstacles which throw us back to waiting on the Lord.

In looking at examples in Scripture where individuals did the will of God, we find that they usually fit this pattern. Paul, for instance, generally assumed that he should take initiative to open doors except for those occasional times when God clearly closed them (Acts 16:6-7, 39-40).

Speaking Our Mind

We can expect, too, that this personal initiative will frequently require us to express our convictions clearly with people—even with those who disagree with us—and that God will use this assertiveness to persuade them and open important doors for us. It is here that we are called to be assertive in the most conventional sense. While we must always listen carefully to the counsel others give us and be open to having our insights changed by theirs, we must realize that God will also use us to counsel them and at times to correct their misunderstandings. We need to become comfortable with this interactive process. We cannot simply assume that God will always want us to acquiesce if others are not immediately in favor of our plans. While we need to be considerate and compassionate when asserting ourselves at such times, we should not be reluctant to express our convictions.

We find a wonderfully instructive example of such bold but courteous assertiveness in the biblical account of David interacting with Saul over fighting Goliath. David took the initiative to propose to Saul that he battle the giant. Saul's initial response was negative: "You are not able to go out against this Philistine and fight him; you are only a boy, and he has been a fighting man from his youth" (1 Sam 17:33). Most would have taken this admonition from the most respected warrior in the land not only as wise counsel but as a glorious pardon from responsibility! David now had an easy out. He had done his duty, declared his willingness to go into the heat of battle, but was told he could stay on the sidelines. He could have his cake and eat it too. He could glory in being the only person to volunteer to fight the giant, yet enjoy the freedom of not having to face the challenge.

But David pressed his point with Saul:

Your servant has been keeping his father's sheep. When a lion or a bear came and carried off a sheep from the flock, I went after it, struck it and rescued the sheep from its mouth. When it turned on me, I seized it by its hair, struck it and killed it. Your servant has killed both the lion and the bear; this uncircumcised Philistine will be like one of them, because he has defied the armies of the living God. The LORD who delivered me from the paw of the lion and the paw of the bear will deliver me from the hand of this Philistine. (1 Sam 17:34-37)

Interestingly, Saul was not put off by David's straightforwardness. To the contrary, he was changed by it. His response: "Go, and the LORD be with you" (1 Sam 17:37). Even after that, David continued to be respectfully assertive with Saul. He urged that he be allowed to fight Goliath without the cumbersome armor Saul thought he needed, and again Saul conceded. If David had taken the "easy out" and passively accepted Saul's advice, he would have stifled his own development—and in addition, a nation of people would have suffered for his silence. This is, in my impression, the most helpful example we find in Scripture of healthy assertiveness. We see God honoring the efforts of one man to convince an individual considerably more knowledge-able and powerful than himself that he has gifts which should be recognized and put to use. An entire nation benefited from his straightforwardness.

The passage drives home a vital point for each of us. Not only does God bring us to see broader opportunities for investing our lives, but he uses us as agents of change to bring these options about. Walking in faith requires that we assert ourselves. We can find the courage to do this if we believe that God will honor our efforts and that others will benefit from our initiative. David's example gives us rich encouragement at this point.

Pacing Yourself

In taking personal initiative, there are two cautions which I would offer. One is that we should consider a step of faith only if we can pursue it without frenzy, within the time and energy limits the Lord has given us and without jeopardizing other commitments we have already made. The other is that our understanding of what steps of faith we should take should grow out of a regular—preferably daily—time alone with Christ, where we carefully think through the direction of our life and what God wants us to do. In general, individuals in Scripture were judged presumptuous not because they took personal initiative but because they did so without establishing their plans before the Lord (Josh 9:14).

As we daily seek the Lord's direction, we should feel great freedom to take bold initiative to find the best opportunities for using our gifts and building relationships. I remember what great relief I felt as a young Christian when my friend told me that it was okay to do this. I hope that you will feel similar relief in realizing the freedom Scripture gives us at this point. The fact is God gives us greater control to change the circumstances of our lives than we tend to think.

Chapter Fifteen

Learning Optimism

After my father-in-law, Glenn Kirkland, lost his wife of forty-six years, Grace, to Alzheimer's disease three years ago, he decided to open himself to getting married again. While finding a suitable spouse is no small challenge for anyone, it is a particularly daunting one for a retired man of seventy-one.

Yet Glenn took the important step of getting socially active again. He began attending a Bible study and joined the large choir at Fourth Presbyterian Church. And from time to time he took initiative, asking a woman to have dinner with him. His first effort at a relationship proved disappointing. After one date, a fifty-five-year-old woman who sparked his interest wrote to him, explaining that she could not go out with him again. The reason: their age difference was simply too great.

But then he met Barbara Nielson. This fifty-eight-year-old psychologist had recently joined Fourth Church and become active in the choir. Things blossomed between them, and after several months of courtship they married. Their relationship is a gem and has brought a new lease on life to both of them in many ways.

I believe there are a number of reasons behind Glenn and Barbara's wonderful marriage. At the top of the list is the grace of God, working to bring them together and convince them of the benefit of marrying. Yet Glenn's optimism also played a vital role and put him in position to receive this gift of God. His belief that he could find someone to marry led him to do the very things which allowed God's provision. The same is true for Barbara; her optimism and sense of adventure positioned her to meet Glenn as well.

I talk with many Christians who would dearly like to be married or to realize some other significant goal, yet are convinced their prospects for success are nil. Their fear of failure is so pervasive that it blocks them from making even the first efforts, and so it becomes a self-fulfilling prophecy. They need a clear perspective for confronting their fear and for answering those internal messages which keep announcing, "This is impossible."

Such a perspective should accomplish two things for us. First, it should give us a reasonable hope for success. Having this hope is vital if we're to find the incentive to begin moving toward our goal. Second, it should give us a healthy attitude toward failure itself. Failure is seldom the monster it pretends to be; indeed, it has its positive side. Appreciating this fact helps us feel more comfortable in the face of taking risks.

A Basis for Hope

When our fears of failure are strong, we need first and foremost to remind ourselves that *our apprehensions may not be in line with reality.* The possibility is very real that we will *not* fail. I personally find it helpful to reflect on incidents like my first phone call for a date to remind myself how unbelievably unrealistic my expectations of doom usually have been. If my predictions of failure have been wrong in the past, they are probably wrong now. I find it helpful, too, to use the thought-stopping technique we have looked at to put a halt to obsessive musings about failure.

Once we have carefully and prayerfully decided upon a particular course of action, we should remind ourselves, "I'm not going to expect failure here. It's not a sure thing that I'm going to fail. It's very possible I will succeed!" Call this positive thinking, if you will. The point comes where it's an essential attitude for the Christian.

What I'm recommending, though, differs from popular ideas about positive thinking in two important ways. First, I'm not suggesting that we should blindly anticipate success even when there is no basis in fact for expecting it. Our expectation should be based on a good analysis of all the facts we have and our best understanding of what God wants us to do. Second, I'm not recommending that we should ever assume that success is guaranteed beyond all question. We must always leave room for the fact that we don't know the mind of God for our future. His timetable, as well as his definition of success, may be different from ours.

With these cautions in mind, we still have strong reason for hope in the major steps we take. We have a sound basis for believing that success is a good probability. It's right and proper and healthy for us to be *substantially* optimistic. This optimism is vital for at least three reasons:

1. Optimism gives credit to the power of God. God is at work behind the scenes in our lives in unfathomable ways—for our good. He desires our very best. He isn't our adversary but our friend. As a general principle he desires our success in life, not our failure. A continuing attitude of pessimism shows that underneath I believe that God is against me, not for me. An optimistic spirit grants that God can work in a multitude of ways, including many I have never fathomed, to bring about a positive outcome.

We noted in chapter three that there are only eight instances in the Gospels where Jesus commends the faith of an individual—that is, where he directly compliments someone's faith. In each of these cases, the faith which impressed Jesus had nothing to do with doctrinal belief; it was a supremely optimistic spirit.

In six of these incidents, individuals expected Jesus to perform a healing miracle for them or for someone else (Mt 8:5-13; 15:21-28; Mk 2:1-12; 5:24-34; 10:46-52; Lk 17:11-19). Their expectation was not based on blind faith, for they had all seen or heard of Jesus performing similar miracles. Still they held to their faith in spite of many factors which might have discouraged them. The woman with the hemorrhage, for instance, had been told by doctors for twelve years that she couldn't be healed; blind Bartimaeus was told by the crowd to stop calling for Jesus; the four men who brought their paralyzed friend to Jesus had to lower him through a tiled roof to get through the crowd. In each instance, individuals through their optimism showed a respect for the power of God which was above and beyond the ordinary. It accents the fact that we honor Christ through an optimistic spirit.

2. Optimism shows respect for the ability of judgment which God gives us. Scripture warns us against trusting in our own understanding (Prov 3:5-6). Yet it also tells us that we who have been born again have "the mind of Christ" (1 Cor 2:16). This means that God has given us the capacity for sensible judgment. As we take pains to think through a choice carefully, and do so with prayer and respect for God's will, Christ leads us to a sound decision. Indeed, part of having faith as a Christian is trusting that Christ will enable me to make good decisions. When I'm confident of having made a good decision, I'm naturally confident that the outcome will be positive. Optimism, then, reflects my conviction that God is guiding my decision process.

3. Optimism contributes to my success. Time and again, experiments in the social sciences have shown that the expectation of success has a significant impact upon actual achievement. When

I'm confident of reaching a goal, I'm inspired to work harder to get to it, and I'm more alert to opportunities which will help me move toward it. Also, my confidence inspires others (often without their realizing it) to act in ways that help me reach my goal. I'm not suggesting that we ever should purposely manipulate others against their will to further our own purposes. But if I'm working toward a goal which Christ has inspired within me, then I'll best allow him to motivate others to help me when my attitude is optimistic.

By the same token, when we expect failure, we easily and subtly end up doing the very things which bring it about. The servant who hid his talent is a classic example of this. He was so afraid of a negative outcome that he did the very thing that would bring about his downfall (Mt 25:14-30). It was the optimistic servants who invested their talents and realized both success and the praise of their master. We should realize that for Christians optimism is not only okay but desirable when taking major steps. This is part of what faith is about. When we have taken reasonable steps to make a careful decision, we should also take reasonable steps to keep our heart expectant as we work toward our goal. If we need to exercise some thought control, we should do so. We shouldn't regard this as falsely "psyching ourselves up" but as good stewardship of our mental process.

We should confront the fear of failure with constant reminders that God desires our best and that we have good reason to be hopeful of reaching our goal.

The Positive Side of Failure

Yes, we fear failure. But the bite of fear is remarkably lessened once we're persuaded that even if the worst occurred, it wouldn't be so bad after all. There are actually significant benefits which failure can bring to us. Understanding these will not only reduce our anxiety about it but also give us fresh heart to try again if disappointment does occur.

While we shouldn't court failure or overtly desire it, neither should we harbor unreasonable apprehensions about it. It's these fears which stifle us from taking steps of faith. We can find the courage to take these steps once we realize that even if failure should occur, we will still benefit from the experience and be better off than if we had simply sat still.

In reality, failure not only helps us grow in important ways but contributes to our long-range experience of success when we know how to accept it and appropriate its benefits. There are at least three ways in which this can happen:

1. *Through failure we learn how to be successful.* The most obvious benefit of failure is that through it our experience grows. Through a hands-on experience we learn in a most authentic way how *not* to do something. Lessons gleaned from experience generally stick with us much better and are much more beneficial than those merely learned academically. If we apply what we have learned to our future experience, our possibility of success is increased significantly.

In eighth grade I had a devastating experience. A musical combo I directed was to play for a school talent show. We had done so the year before, and though our music was terrible the students gave us a tumultuous response. As a result, we were scheduled this time to conclude the assembly. We fully expected to give a top performance and to be counted as class heroes for the rest of the year.

We walked on stage to tremendous applause, our heads swelling with pride. But shortly after we began our first number, sound stopped coming forth from my guitar amplifier. I looked down and realized that the wires connecting the guitar cord to the amp jack had pulled loose. An electric guitar without amplification is about as useful as a TV set not turned on, and since I was the only melody instrument in the group, we had no choice but to stop the song. I bent down and for several anxious minutes struggled to reattach the wires, but in my frenzy only succeeded in snapping them off the cord. As I fumbled with the cord, the students became noisy and unruly. Finally I looked up to see the gargantuan figure of the school principal stepping up to the microphone. He proceeded to chastise the students for their rowdiness and ordered them back to class.

Far from treating us as heroes, for the next few weeks our classmates looked on us as stooges who kept them from having a good time. The shame and humiliation that we felt was incredible.

In time, however, I came to count this experience as one of the most beneficial of my life. Through it I discovered in a most unforgettable way the need for preparation. When a cord would break in a later performance, there was an extra one there to replace it. And in many ways the experience touched my life and gave me the incentive to go an extra mile in getting ready for the things I do. No textbook could have taught me the lesson as well.

Most of us, if we'll look honestly at our lives, will admit that certain hard experiences have done much to teach us and equip us for the quality of life we now live. Failures in relationships have taught us how to relate to people better. Failures in academic and work experiences have taught us how to approach certain types of work more effectively. Failures in parenting have taught us how to better encourage and guide our children. Business failures have given us a wiser approach to investments. Moral and spiritual defeat has taught us how to draw more fully on the power of Christ. Through all of these experiences we have come to understand our own gifts, strengths and weaknesses better, and that in turn has given us a more confident grasp of God's direction in our lives.

These experiences can benefit us *if* we can take them in the right spirit. Some discouragement is normal when failure and disappointment come, and we need to allow ourselves the freedom to grieve significant losses and setbacks. Yet the point comes where we need to begin to take a more positive look at our failure and see what beneficial lessons can be gained from it. The danger is that we get paralyzed by our failure. We assume that failure once means failure forever. We conclude that God is against us and has shown us our fate through this unhappy experience. We lose the courage to try again.

An experience of the Israelites recorded in Joshua 7 is particularly instructive for us here. The Jews under Joshua had experienced many military victories and became headstrong. They decided to take on the city of Ai with only a few thousand soldiers, greatly underestimating their opponents' strength. And they didn't know that one of their number, Achan, had taken some "devoted" items from a previous battle that God had commanded destroyed, thus arousing God's wrath against Israel.

The men of Ai chased back Israel's army and killed thirty-six men, a relatively minor defeat. But we're told that "the hearts of the [Israelites] melted and became like water" (v. 5). Then Joshua, devastated, wallows on the ground and prays,

Ah, Sovereign LORD, why did you ever bring this people across the Jordan to deliver us into the hands of the Amorites to destroy us? . . . The Canaanites and the other people of the country will hear about this and they will surround us and wipe out our name from the earth. (Josh 7:7, 9)

God does not debate Joshua's reflections but gives him practical instructions: he is to rid Israel of the one who has taken the devoted things. Joshua obeys. Then God tells him to take *all* the fighting men and attack Ai again. This time Israel has a resounding victory.

The Israelites gained two immeasurable benefits from their defeat with Ai: a deeper awareness of where they were vulnerable to sin against God and a sharper understanding of the logistics necessary to rout a formidable foe. When they repented and put their new insights into action, they became remarkably successful at a point of previous failure. Yet reaching this point meant getting beyond the wallowing stage. At first all Joshua could see was his failure, and all hope for further success eluded him. It was only when he got beyond this point and listened to God's perspective that he realized this mortifying defeat could contribute to future victory.

When failure comes, we're too often tempted to remain at the wallowing stage. Like Joshua, we cannot see past our failure, and all our thoughts are colored by it. At such times we must put into practice everything we know about repentance and the grace and forgiveness of Christ. But we must also take into account everything we know about the creative power of God. He is speaking to us as with Joshua, telling us to learn what we can from our failure and move on. And when we do, we find that vital growth has come through the experience which could not have come any other way. A friend of mine sums it up by saying that one of our main concerns in life should be to learn to be a "successful failure." This principle will serve us well both in the face of actual failure and as we anticipate the risks involved in taking a step of faith.

2. *Failure can carry a success of its own.* A second point to remember is that experiences which we initially perceive to be failures sometimes in the end turn out to be successes. We find we called the shots wrong. Our sense that we have been a total flop can keep us from noticing successes which may be part of a situation.

Christian psychiatrist Paul Tournier writes about one of his most humiliating experiences, which occurred when he was giving a talk at a university:

> I felt right from the first word that I was not going to make contact with my audience. I clung to my notes and laboriously recited, with growing nervousness, what I had to say. As the audience left I could see my friends slipping hurriedly away. . . . On the way home in my car with my wife, I burst into tears.[1]

The next day a professor of philosophy phoned him and said that the talk was indeed the worst he had ever heard. But he added that while he had sat through numerous erudite lectures in his lifetime which had left no impression on him, somehow he was drawn to Tournier. A lasting friendship between the two developed, one which resulted in the professor's coming to Christ. Tournier now looks back upon that awful lecture as one of the great successes of his life.

Tournier's experience reminds us that failure can have more than just educational value. The failure may in fact be a success which we don't yet recognize. There are times when we fail to live up to our own expectations but fulfill God's quite well. The experience we perceive to be a failure may indeed be a success in his mind, contributing in a most positive way to our future and to his intentions for our life. God understands success much better than we do.

Tournier's experience also brings out how God honors our honest efforts at success, often in ways that go considerably beyond our initial perceptions. It's fitting, too, to reflect here on the experience of Jesus himself. His brief mission to earth was judged at the end, by friends and foes alike, to have failed. Today we know it was the greatest victory of all time. It stands forth as an example of God's capacity to bring success out of apparent failure.

3. It sometimes takes a certain number of failures to bring about a success. The final benefit of failure we need to look at is more mystical and difficult to pin down. Yet it's no less important to understand. There seems to be a law in human life that success comes about only through a number of earnest attempts. It sometimes takes a number of failures to breed a success. It is the principle of casting seeds which is talked about so frequently in Scripture. Some seeds take root while others do not, for reasons we never fully understand. Yet the greater the number sown, the greater the likelihood of a rich harvest. Thus, Scripture declares,

As you do not know the path of the wind, or how the body is formed in a mother's womb, so you cannot understand the

work of God, the Maker of all things. Sow your seed in the
morning, and at evening let not your hands be idle, for you
do not know which will succeed, whether this or that, or
whether both will do equally well. (Eccles 11:5-6)

Sometimes, yes, failure does mean we made mistakes. As we
examine our experience, we discover what we did wrong and
how to avoid these errors in the future. We learn from our failure
and grow through it. Yet in other cases we are not able to discern
clear mistakes. Our failure seems to have come about in spite of
our doing everything right. At such times we are especially prone
to self-disparagement, for the evidence seems to suggest that
God has cast the lots against us. We become fatalistic and conclude that God doesn't want us to succeed in this particular area.
We lose the courage to try again.

The fact is we don't know the mind of God. Usually we have
very little basis for judging whether he is punishing us through
a failure or not. The possibility is just as real that the failure
suggests only that God's time for success has not yet come for us.
The principle of seed-casting isn't less likely now, but *more* so! If
we'll simply keep casting the seeds, eventually one will take root.
It's fair to think of this, too, as a principle of compensation.
Failure with one try is compensated for by success with another.

Genesis records a time when Isaac and his servants made three
attempts to dig for water in the valley of Gerar (Gen 26:19-22).
After each of the first two, native herdsmen quarreled with them
over property rights, and Isaac's men had to abandon the wells
after all the hard work of digging them. But the third time they
were successful and there was no resistance. Isaac named the well
Rehoboth ("a broad place"), declaring, "Now the LORD has given
us room and we will flourish in the land." Less hardy souls would
have given up after the first or second attempt, saying, "God
doesn't intend that I succeed."

Another example which fascinates me is a fishing incident
involving Jesus' disciples in John 21. John relates that they

fished all night but caught nothing. In the morning Jesus appeared on the lakeside and told them to cast their net on the right side of the boat. They obeyed and hauled in a net bulging with fish. What is interesting is that Jesus didn't tell them to do anything different from what they had been doing all along. They had undoubtedly thrown the net over the right side of the boat many times during that long, futile night of fishing. What made the difference now was the fact that *Jesus* commanded them to do it. This doesn't mean they had been out of his will or doing anything wrong up to this point, but simply that he had not yet intended them to be successful.

The principle of casting seeds seems to be an aspect of God's common grace, a means of his dealing with all people, and one which touches humanity at all points of pursuit. In their book *In Search of Excellence,* Thomas Peters and Robert Waterman note that repeated effort is one of the most common keys to success among notable businesses. The oil companies that are most successful in discovering oil, for instance, are not the ones with the best equipment or the most intelligent personnel but the ones that dig the most wells! Persistence is the factor which separates successful firms from unsuccessful ones.[2]

Yet the principle is also one that applies to the Christian's walk of faith. Even a man as spiritually mature as the apostle Paul at times had to make several bungled attempts before he finally experienced a successful opening to use his gifts for Christ (Acts 16:6-10).

This is perhaps the most important principle to keep in mind in reference to romantic relationships. I have counseled with many older singles who have gone through several disappointments and are now ready to throw in the towel. They are convinced that their chances of marrying are nonexistent and that failures in the past must prove God has not cut them out for marriage. Seldom do I believe that this conclusion is justified. In the immensely complex world of romantic relationships, the chemistry may not work in one case—but then it may do so wonderfully and surprisingly in another. God's timetable with each of us is remarkably different, and we shouldn't assume that disappointment in the past means we're doomed to disappointment forever. There may be lessons to be learned from past experience. But in many cases the failure of romance to flourish simply means that the compatibility factors were not right, and nothing you could have done would have changed that (in which case, you may have been saved from a very difficult marriage!). In another relationship the mix of factors will be quite different and compatibility may be much more natural.

When disappointment in romance comes we should, to be sure, pray that God will give us a heart to accept our present situation joyfully. But praying for acceptance of the present is not incompatible with praying for change in the future. If the desire for marriage continues to be strong, you should be honest in expressing it to God and continue to be hopeful that the opportunity will come about.

In romance and in other areas too, we need to be careful not to fall into a fatalistic mentality about the future due to past failure. Particularly when there are no clear lessons to be learned from failure, the principle of seed-casting suggests that we should stay hopeful. Failure in the past may indicate we are now in line for a victory. The important thing is not to lose heart. We must not close the door in any area of our life before God is ready to do so.

Chapter Sixteen

Playing a Role— and Staying Whole

A *few weeks ago I made my periodic visit to the Hallmark* store, a sojourn that seems to become more periodic with each year of life! To me buying greeting cards is serious business. There is no eenie-meenie-minie-mo about it; finding the card that fits the person and the occasion is critical.

The down side is that I agonize over the whole process more than I should and would be embarrassed to admit how much time I can spend combing the racks to find the perfect card. It will come as no surprise that other members of my family happily delegate the mission of card buying to me. This leaves me particularly burdened on those occasions when multiple cards must be purchased for multiple family members.

On this day there were nine to purchase, covering the upcoming Mother's Day and the birthday of Barbara, my wife's stepmom. Fortunately I got through the task in record time, and in about twenty minutes dumped a stack of cards on the checkout counter. The salesclerk meticulously sorted through them, making certain there was an envelope to match each card. She then looked up at me and exclaimed effusively, "Wow, you picked out a lot of cards. Congratulations, sir!"

Congratulations? I cannot remember ever being so enthusiastically commended for such an ordinary retail purchase before. *Surely she doesn't mean it,* I thought; *this is just a knee-jerk "have-a-nice-day" response, like the free potpourri she threw in the bag.* Yet she seemed sincere enough. And as she totaled the charges ($22.00), I realized there had been creative effort involved in picking out those cards. It felt nice to be complimented for such a routine task. Frankly, we all need a lot more affirmation for the small accomplishments of life than we usually receive.

It is in this spirit that I want to say congratulations for finishing this book. While reading a book from start to finish may not seem like a major achievement, it does in fact take some definite discipline and focus to do so. If you're like me, your shelves contain many books that you bought with the best intentions of reading them but that have only collected dust. Others were indulged for a few chapters, then set aside for a rainy day that never came. Completing a book *is* an accomplishment. Congratulations!

Congratulations are due on another level, for if you picked up this book with the hope of gaining victory over shyness, I can assure you that you have already set the wheels in motion. Whether or not you agree with every point I have made, the process of working through this book in itself has caused you to rethink your perspective at different points and to consider new ways of becoming more outgoing. You have taken an important step forward, even if just on the conceptual level. You don't have to lose that momentum now. This can be the push which moves you into more confident social encounters and a fuller realizing of your personal potential.

If you have already taken some of the steps suggested in this book, then double congratulations are in order. As small as these beginnings may seem, they are very significant, for you have proven to yourself that you do not have to be restricted by your fears. These have been courageous steps on your part. Don't lose heart now but continue the effort. I commend you (sorry I cannot send you a free potpourri).

Seeing the Red Flags

As we begin to work at becoming more outgoing, it helps to be aware of the resistance our psyche may give us. In this concluding chapter, I want to look at a challenge you will likely face as positive changes begin to take place in your life.

As we make any serious effort to master our shyness—be it to control our fears, to improve our social skills, to put ourselves in a better position to meet people and build relationships, to make advances in our profession, to become more assertive, or to change our patterns of pessimistic thinking—we are likely to be troubled at times with the feeling of being less than genuine in adopting the new behavior or identity. "Smiling at this person on purpose just isn't me," you may say. Or, "Being assertive with this pushy salesperson just doesn't fit with who I am." While on one level we may want to do these things, on another level we feel artificial.

Some find that the feeling of being a fake continues to trouble them even long after they succeed in changing their behavior or in reaching some cherished goal in relationships, career or other areas. This is a problem faced by many nonshy individuals as well as shy people. But the problem can be especially severe for the shy person, given the level of change often involved in moving forward.

If we are not to lose heart in the effort to overcome our inhibitions, it is important that we be prepared for the self-doubt and false guilt that can accompany the effort—and know how to respond to it. This challenge can be met, if we have a clear-headed understanding of how our psyche adjusts to personal growth and change, and a broad-minded view of what constitutes the "authentic self." Without this perspective, we are likely to stay stuck in the inertia of our shyness or be nagged with guilt if we succeed in breaking it.

Feeling like a Fake

Consider these four examples.

☐ Richard pastors a Midwestern community church which he helped to found eight years ago. During this time the fledgling congregation has grown to several hundred members and features a dynamic ministry. Richard was a successful businessman in the community before changing his vocation to pastoral ministry. Inside he still *feels* more like a businessman than a pastor. Almost weekly he becomes frustrated as he struggles to formulate a meaningful sermon for his people, a task that continues to feel unnatural to him. He worries that his attitude falls short of the serenity that should characterize a pastor. The fact that he has to work so hard at producing an effective sermon convinces him, too, that his faith is not as strong as it should be.

Overall, Richard still feels like a fish out of water in his pastoral identity, even after eight years of fruitful ministry. He is considering leaving the pastorate altogether and even confessing to his congregation that he has been play-acting to a large extent these past eight years.

Ironically, his congregation is extremely pleased with his ministry and especially with the depth of his preaching. No one seems the least bit concerned that there might be some dichotomy between his public and private images.

☐ Sheryl is a corporation lawyer in Atlanta. Though her work is esteemed by her colleagues, she finds it hard to reconcile her successful white-collar image with her poor rural upbringing. In her self-image she still sees herself as a poor farm girl. The first in her family to finish college, let alone grad school, she continues to feel that she is out of her element. She worries that others will see her as a fake or that something will happen to expose her to the world as incompetent.

☐ Betsy and Henry have dated for three years. They have a supportive, compassionate relationship. They have talked often and enthusiastically about marriage, and Henry is convinced Betsy would be ideal for him. Betsy, though, sometimes feels that she is just going through the motions in their relationship—and that worries her. There are times when she simply doesn't feel supportive of Henry, and times when the romantic sizzle doesn't seem as strong as it should be. Though on one level Betsy wants to be married, she wonders if she is really cut out for a romantic relationship. Sometimes the role seems alien to her independent nature.

☐ Jason is father of three children, ages nine, six and four. Those who know him regard him as an excellent parent, and indeed he makes a noble effort to give his kids the attention they need. Yet he confesses that the task of parenting still feels like "too much too soon" for him. He doesn't feel like a parent but more like a kid at heart. *His* parents—*they* are the real parents. The role of parent seems distant from how he thinks of himself.

Richard, Sheryl, Betsy and Jason each suffer from an attitude of self-judgment which psychologist Joan Harvey terms the "impostor phenomenon." In *If I'm So Successful, Why Do I Feel Like a Fake?*[1] she describes the plight of numerous individuals who have achieved success in various areas yet are plagued with fear that they are not truly qualified for the positions or status they have attained. They worry that others have been fooled, duped into thinking they are more capable than they really are. They attribute their success to some factor other than true ability: luck, availability, charm, personality, hard work, parental influence, tokenism or an employer's need to fill a quota. They look upon themselves as frauds and live in fear of others' discovering their true colors. These are people, Harvey stresses, who are not genuine impostors but are adept in their areas of accomplishment; still they are obsessed with fears of being incompetent.

We who are shy almost always struggle with impostor feelings when we achieve success as well as when we make any effort to change our behavior or improve our lives. Our tendency to analyze and our heightened fear of how people will judge us make us prone to worry that others will think we are fraudulent. Often, too, we are inordinately conscious of mixed motives and fear that God is displeased with us.

Roles and Ideals

One of the factors which makes us subject to impostor feelings, Harvey notes, is that we have to take on roles in life—roles which sometimes do not fit perfectly with the self-images we have long held. Some find assuming *any* role painfully uncomfortable. They are so concerned with being authentic and true to their inner self that any change in outward identity seems unnatural. An example is someone who always feels inauthentic wearing different modes of dress and so wears the same apparel for formal and informal occasions alike.

Others feel comfortable in some roles but uneasy with others, even with some roles which others believe fit them quite well. This is true for each of the four individuals mentioned above. They are trying to accommodate themselves to roles which they fear do not fully reflect their authentic personhood or potential. The result is a feeling of fraudulence, which drains their energy and makes them doubt they are where God really wants them.

Concern among psychologists with the challenge of accommodating ourselves to roles is not new. Christian psychiatrist Paul Tournier wrote a groundbreaking and probing book on the subject in 1957, entitled *The Meaning of Persons.*[2] Tournier notes that life requires us to take on a number of "personas," or "personages," which can never perfectly reflect our true inner self. Anxiety and guilt over the fear of deceiving others often result. While Tournier does not use the term "impostor phenomenon," which was coined in the 1970s by Harvey, his concerns are similar to hers in many ways.

As Christians we are especially vulnerable to feeling fraudulent in new roles, given our acute awareness of the inner sinful nature and the critical need for truthfulness in everything we do. "Thou desirest truth in the inward being," David declares in Psalm 51:6 (RSV). It can seem that the assuming of any role forces us to appear to the world contrary to how we really are—and thus to violate the biblical requirement for thoroughgoing honesty.

Add to this the sheer number of roles we *have* to assume in any short period of time. In the past week alone I have taken on the roles of teacher, pastor, counselor, writer, song leader, student, husband, father, son, son-in-law, shopper, homemaker, letter writer, customer, friend, neighbor, restaurant patron, driver, businessperson (negotiating for yard work), computer hack (looking into equipment needed for the ministry), musical performer (planning for a presentation by our family), and member of a congregation (sitting through a worship service)—just to mention the ones that come to mind quickly. I'm sure your situation is no different; you find yourself assuming numerous roles not only in a typical week but in a typical day. For the sensitive, thinking Christian, there is a constant struggle in reconciling who you really are with how you must appear to others.

Adjusting Our Self-Image

Fortunately, both Harvey and Tournier have redemptive advice to offer for this struggle. Harvey stresses that we need to redefine our concept of the self. We are too inclined to think of ourselves in terms of one facet of our life or personality. "I'm a homemaker." Or, "I'm an accountant." Or, "I'm an artist." Instead, Harvey argues, we should come to see ourselves as *multidimensional,* or *multifaceted.* We need to learn to think of ourselves in terms of our total mix of roles and functions, to become comfortable identifying with any of them and with moving in and out of each of them as the situation requires. This is not a denial of our authentic self but simply a different way of understanding what the human self actually is.

Harvey warns, too, that we must be careful not to fall into an idealized self-image as we take on different roles. Too often, when we rate ourselves as fraudulent in a certain role we are judging ourselves by an unrealistic standard which in reality no one could live up to. When a woman like Betsy fears she is being inauthentic in a relationship because her romantic feelings vary at times, she misses the fact that these feelings are *never* consistent. There is always an ebb and flow to romantic emotions, even in the best relationships—even in a good marriage. The important thing is to look at the overall pattern of feelings over time.

Harvey also makes the helpful observation that impostor feelings are most likely to strike when we take on a new role. The shy person, for example, who decides to make a concerted effort to be more personable and assertive will at first feel he is being less than authentic in his manner of relating to others. Yet eventually his new approach to people starts to feel natural; he begins to own his new behavior and stops feeling he is merely playing a role, just as the skills of tennis or driving a car become second nature when practiced enough.

Tournier also stresses that we need to redefine how we think of the self and what it means to be an authentic person. While we each have a distinctive inner personhood, we cannot strip away the outward personas—like peeling off the outer layers of an onion—and expect to finally discover the true inner core of the self. Indeed, our personhood is reflected *through* the roles which we take on and cannot be understood apart from them. The key is to choose those personas which best reflect the individual we truly are. Tournier notes,

> We must resign ourselves to this indissoluble connection between . . . the person and its personages. For we are not only

one personage throughout our lives; we are innumerable personages. At each new encounter we show ourselves different; with one friend we are the serious thinker; with another, the wag; we change our demeanor to suit each new situation. We are even many personages at once. . . .

The tension that always exists between the person and the personage is one of the conditions of our life, and we must accept it. It is part of the nature of man—indeed, it is what makes him a man.[3]

The Biblical Perspective

When we turn to Scripture, we find interesting support for the conclusions which Harvey and Tournier reach, and many further helpful insights besides.

To begin with, the Scriptures stress emphatically that genuine impostors do exist, and warnings about them permeate the Bible. (*"Genuine* impostors?" Well, that's the limitation of our language!) There are numerous examples of false prophets, cagey magicians, unscrupulous rulers and religious leaders who use the guise of spiritual power to dominate others and further their own selfish ends. Jesus minces no words in condemning those who are real impostors and in warning us to beware of their menace:

> Beware of the teachers of the law. They like to walk around in flowing robes and love to be greeted in the marketplaces and have the most important seats in the synagogues and the places of honor at banquets. They devour widows' houses and for a show make lengthy prayers. Such men will be punished most severely. (Lk 20:46-47)

On a less condemning note, there are also examples in Scripture of individuals who with good intentions entertained taking on roles which were not truly suited to their individuality. There is David who with all his heart wanted to build the temple for God. Yet God responded that David did not have the right temperament for the task, which was to await the reign of his son, Solomon (1 Chron 17:3-12; 22:6-10). Then there is the demon-possessed man from the Gerasenes whom Jesus healed, who wanted to travel with Jesus; Jesus responded that he should instead return to his home town and tell everyone there what Jesus had done for him (Lk 8:38-39).

But at the other extreme, the Bible is flooded with examples of individuals who fulfilled God's will by taking on various roles—roles which probably did not seem fully natural to them at first and in some cases may never have. There are graphic instances where individuals were clearly uncomfortable with the early stages of a role into which God called them. Moses and Jeremiah were both frightened of public speaking (Ex 4:10-13; Jer 1:6; *terrified* is probably the better word in Moses' case). As we have noted, Gideon suffered from such low self-esteem that he was incredulous at the angel's assertion that he was the right man to lead Israel's army against Midian (Judg 6:15). We infer from the various times that Paul exhorted Timothy not to be afraid, to rekindle his gift or to apply himself to his pastoral task, that Timothy was timid in his pastoral identity and may well have suffered some impostor feelings—this in spite of the fact that he is set forth as the prototype of a good pastor in the New Testament! (See, for instance, 1 Tim 4:12, 14-15; 5:23; 2 Tim 1:7-8; compare 1 Cor 16:10.)

While Moses, Jeremiah and Gideon seem to have gotten over their initial uneasiness as they became acclimated to their roles, Timothy apparently continued to feel insecure and needed frequent propping up from Paul. It is interesting, though, that God never allowed these men to cave in to the awkwardness they felt; it was never a reason to assume they were not qualified in God's sight to carry out the role in question.

It is in the same spirit that the New Testament exhorts us in various places to understand our gifts and to give our closest attention to developing and using them. To do so invariably requires assuming some new roles, both as we cultivate a gift and as we apply it in new situations. The chances are good we will experience some impostor feelings as we adjust to new roles and identities that are not yet natural to us. Yet never does the New Testament tell us to hold back from using our gifts because of these feelings. Rather we are told emphatically, "If our gift is preaching, let us preach to the limit of our vision. If it is serving others let us concentrate on our service; if it is teaching let us give all we have to our teaching; and if our gift be the stimulating of the faith of others let us set ourselves to it" (Rom 12:6-8 Phillips).

And in case there is any doubt that it is okay for us as Christians to assume different personas in different situations, there is the extreme example of Paul, who proclaimed, "I have become all things to all men so that by all possible means I might save some" (1 Cor 9:22). We have evidence that Paul sometimes felt profoundly uneasy in roles he took on (1 Cor 2:3-5). While he never declared that all believers are required to go to his extreme of adapting to diverse cultural situations, his example does suggest convincingly that *some* modifying of our outward persona not only is permitted but will probably be needed as we seek to realize our full potential for Christ.

Role Playing in Scripture

I like those instances in Scripture where individuals actually did play-act in order to make a point or accomplish a goal, fooling others in the process, yet are not presented as out of God's will in doing so. There is the moving episode where Joseph's brothers come to him in Egypt to seek grain during a famine, and for some time he does not let on that he is their long-abandoned sibling but lets them assume he is merely an Egyptian official (Gen 42:1—45:15). Then there is the incident where the prophet Nathan, with a straight face, tells David a fabricated story of a rich man who has stolen a poor man's only possession, a beloved ewe lamb, as a creative technique for leading David to a point of personal brokenness over his stealing Bathsheba and arranging for the murder of her husband (2 Sam 12:1-12).

Or consider the occasion where David pretends to be insane in order to escape capture by King Achish—foaming at the mouth and scratching at a gate with his hands (1 Sam 21:12-15). Here he acts in an unquestionably deceptive manner, and we might think he had to be violating God's perfect will in doing so. Yet, intriguingly, David wrote Psalm 34 to celebrate the victory God gave him in this incident, and in that psalm he shows no remorse for his play-acting but implies that through it God enabled him to escape capture by a tyrant. Particularly interesting is the fact that he also declares in this psalm, "Keep your tongue from evil, and your lips from speaking deceit" (v. 13 RSV). This would suggest that he did not think of feigning madness in this case as inconsistent with living a life free of deceit.

Of course, the lesson of the incident is not that we have a license to behave in a deceptive way toward others as our general manner of lifestyle. But the possibility is not ruled out by Scripture, either, at least in certain extreme situations where we might be dealing with a fundamentally cruel or irrational person, and where our own safety or someone else's might be at stake (compare Prov 26:4-5).

But in a more general way we can take encouragement from David's example of feigning madness, simply because it is so extreme compared to the role situations where we typically judge ourselves as fraudulent. I think this incident helps us put our own situations in more healthy perspective and jars us into realizing that our own "role playing" is usually mild by comparison with the level of play-acting involved in this case. And David apparently was not acting contrary to God's will.

Living Boldly

In short, we need to learn to live the Christian life courageously.

On the one hand, we need to examine ourselves very honestly, seeking to understand our own hearts and motives as thoroughly as possible. We need to boldly ask God to do whatever is needed to purify our intentions and to make our hearts pliable before him. As we come to recognize ways in which we are clearly living in a deceptive manner or disregarding Christ's standards, we must make the changes that are needed.

At the same time, we need just as courageously to take bold steps to realize our potential for Christ. We need to seek to understand our gifts and temperament as best as we can, to strive to develop our abilities, and to look for the best opportunities available for investing our gifts and for developing relationships. We should accept that in this process we will probably experience some impostor feelings at times, for with personal growth invariably come some journeys through untrodden territory. The fact that we *feel* less than authentic in a role does not necessarily mean we are sinning, acting contrary to God's will or violating our true inner self. It may simply be that we are not living up to our own unrealistic standards. There are times when we fail to live up to our own ideals and yet fulfill God's quite well.

Even when our motives are less than perfect, we usually give God the best opportunity to purify them as we stay in motion. God's pattern for the Christian life is that we do take on some roles. Here we need to make the best choices we can and move on. I agree with Tournier:

Instead of turning our backs on the outside world and concentrating on our own inner life, where the true nature of the person always eludes us, we must look outward, toward the world, toward our neighbor, toward God. We must boldly undertake the formation of a personage for ourselves, seeking to form it in accordance with our sincerest convictions, so that it will express and show forth the person that we are.[4]

One final point. While Scripture provides us plenty of basis for perhaps the greatest incentive comes from one overriding fact—that of the Incarnation. By choosing to become man in Jesus Christ, God took on *a role*. He assumed an identity that was foreign to who he had been from the foundation of time—first in the form of a baby and finally in the form of an adult man with all of our humanity (Heb 2:14; 4:15).

As we consider this incomparable truth, may we be inspired with courage to be creative and courageous as we take steps to break the bonds of shyness. May the fact that God became human in Christ encourage us likewise to seek those roles and situations where we may best glorify him through being the individual he has made us to be. We may be shy, but we will reach out to people. We may have doubts about ourselves, but we will rest in God's words, "You are precious and honored in my sight" (Is 43:4). We may feel hesitant to play an uncomfortable role, but we'll do it when it is right. With God's help, we'll overcome the crippling aspects of our shyness—and live free.

Appendix: Tips for Confronting an Audience

Over half of those who took my Shyness Survey indicate they are fearful of public speaking. Others note that they are hampered by stage fright in musical or dramatic performing. While some describe their anxiety as mild, others say it is extreme. Not a few refer to public speaking or performing as the area where their fear of people is most debilitating.

Not all who are shy with individuals are fearful in front of a group. Indeed, it is one of the ironies of shyness that these two do not always go hand in hand. There are chronically shy people who are confident to a fault speaking or performing in front of others. The fact that there is structure and agenda to the performance situation helps them feel comfortable. It is the unpredictability of the informal social situation that makes them nervous. Their confidence with an audience may spring, too, from being specially gifted in speaking or performing.

At the other extreme, there are many gregarious folks who do not consider themselves shy at all, yet suffer considerable "performance anxiety." Indeed, it is here that the popular definition of what it means to be shy begins to break down—or at least needs to be amended a bit. Some who are quite comfortable interacting with people informally will freeze if asked to give a talk in public. Even some who are confident giving a presentation such as a sales pitch to an individual will become unraveled if they have to deliver it to a group of just a few people.

One vivacious woman I know works for a major political association. She so impressed her employers with her interpersonal skills that she was given the task of soliciting contributors—asking each one to donate $1500. She is comfortable and effective in a job which would intimidate most of us. Yet the thought of giving even a brief talk to a small group so unnerves her that she will go to any lengths to avoid it. It took a monumental act of will power for her to give a short report on her activities to her highly supportive Sunday-school class. She was on edge about it for days in advance.

Another friend of mine is a successful salesman of luxury automobiles. I scarcely need to tell you the level of social confidence needed to be effective in this line of work. Yet when elected president of his church fellowship group, he found it unnerving to make even brief introductory remarks at the meetings. At his daughter's wedding he worried incessantly over his only lines in the ceremony—a three-sentence commendation to the bride and groom. He was able to get through this traumatic moment only by reading his comments verbatim from a card.

More Common Than We Think

This fear of confronting an audience is amazingly pervasive. In a national survey, Americans were asked to note their strongest fears. Speaking before a group ranked first; death seventh.[1]

David Sharp, writing for *Health* magazine, observes,

Pick any four people . . . and these are the odds: Two of the four will feel at least an occasional flutter of stage fright before a speech. The third will suffer nervousness that could be called bothersome but not debilitating. And the fourth person will be so fearful that he or she will avoid meetings, drop classes, refuse promotions, or change jobs to escape confronting an audience. For fully a quarter of us, then, the emotional and physiological agony of stage fright can cause us to self-destruct when facing even the most benign crowd.[2]

It can be a revelation to discover just how many well-known, highly successful public personalities suffer significant performance anxiety. While singer Carly Simon's stage fright is legendary, many other singers, such as classical vocalist Cynthia Mahaney, also experience panic while performing. Although Willard Scott speaks openly about his ordeal with stage fright, many who watch the outrageously popular weather anchor have no idea of the agony he goes through to fulfill his role. In fact, Scott admits to daily episodes of severe anxiety, hyperventilation and rapid heartbeat before giving his brief segments on NBC's *Today Show.* Many renowned actors, such as Laurence Olivier, confess to a lifetime battle with chronic stage fright. Acting was so traumatic for Olivier that he forbade other cast members to look him in the eye during a play.

Or consider the case of acclaimed cellist Pablo Casals. "On occasion [he] had to be physically pushed onto the stage. So debilitating was his fear that when a rock fell on Casals' hand during a hike, he announced with great relief, 'Thank God, I'll never have to play cello again.' (Fortunately—at least for his audiences—he recovered.)"[3]

Among the many Christians I know who have struggled with stage fright, some have successfully conquered or outgrown it, while others in spite of their best efforts continue to experience some anxiety in audience situations.

One friend of mine, a forty-nine-year-old man who continues

to be shy in personal relations, notes with glee that stage fright is a thing of the past for him: "A course in public speaking and teaching experiences in Sunday school have caused me to completely overcome the fear of public speaking. It works!"

While many whom I know echo his experience, others would love to give that same testimony but simply can't. In my case, stage fright continues to be a problem even though I have given lectures publicly for twenty-five years and performed music for some time before that. My experience has included many lengthy talks before large and diverse audiences, day-long seminars, weekend retreats, and two recent appearances on live national television. In spite of this level of experience, I continue to be nervous before many talks and especially before ones that I consider to be "major." There have been more Friday nights at weekend conferences than I care to remember when I did not sleep a wink at all.

While this may not sound like a very positive testimony to the possibility of overcoming stage fright, there is a positive side. I have grown more comfortable with many types of audience situations and have learned many techniques which help me on all occasions when I speak. Perhaps most important, I have learned how to deal with the onset of fear and am no longer afraid of fear as I once was. Overall there has been some encouraging improvement. Among Christians I know who struggle with stage fright, I am happy to say that every one who has made a sincere effort to deal with it has made some degree of progress. I am not aware of any who have not at least become able to function acceptably in front of an audience, and some have become surprisingly comfortable in the role.

This accords well with the observation of Peter Desberg, a Los Angeles psychologist who specializes in treating performance anxiety. "I've never worked with a person who didn't improve," he says. "It's an issue of how hard they were willing to work, and where the problem started, and how intense it was."[4]

If stage fright is a significant problem for you, rest assured there is hope. If you make the effort, you will reach the point where it is not nearly so threatening. And with some work you can make substantial improvement in your ability to function comfortably and effectively in front of an audience.

You Can Do It

Depending upon your gifts and aspirations, this effort may be well worth making. I remember talking with a Christian student, an InterVarsity member who was well liked and had obvious gifts for ministry. He had an ardent desire to go to seminary and prepare for pastoral ministry, yet he was holding back for a single reason: he was terrified of public speaking. There are many of us like him, who have put legitimate dreams on hold because of our fear of facing the crowd. Not only is our potential for Christ being thwarted but we are robbing ourselves of a level of fulfillment and joy in our work that we could be experiencing. Be honest with yourself. If performance anxiety is holding you back from realizing your full potential, take steps to confront the problem. The good news is that there *are* steps you can take and through these you can experience significant healing.

I do hope the examples of public figures who experience performance anxiety are encouraging and not disheartening to you. I cite them because we who are bedeviled by stage fright are usually relieved to discover just how universal the problem is. The drawback is that we may think, "If these folks continue to be fearful in spite of all their experience, what hope is there for me?" Keep two things in mind. One is that these people have learned to function effectively in front of a crowd *in spite of* their anxieties. They demonstrate profoundly that we do not have to allow our fears to paralyze us and keep us back from realizing our potential. We *can* feel the fear and do it anyway.

There is another point—a critical point—which is usually overlooked when the experiences of notable people with stage fright are cited. It's the fact that a major reason these people continue to be nervous in front of an audience is that they expose themselves to ever more challenging situations. Willard Scott, for instance, did not have a major problem with stage fright when he was a popular radio personality in Washington, D.C., or when he was a local weather anchor on TV here. It was only after coming to the *Today Show* that the problem began to be serious. And who *wouldn't* be intimidated, to know you have but a minute and a half to be articulate, informative and amusing to an audience of millions of strangers throughout the world who are staring at your face for that brief moment of time? By the same token, I doubt Laurence Olivier in his professional years would have been frightened to act in front of a rural audience of several hundred attending a community players production at a high school. But his career thrust him into some of the most prestigious and intimidating venues in the world. Small wonder stage fright continued to be a problem.

I'm certain that if we asked any of these famous personalities about the *totality* of their experience, they would readily admit that they have made important strides in dealing with stage fright. There are audience situations which used to be intimidating to them in which they are now quite comfortable. They are also better able to manage their fear; it is not as dominant as in the past. We can take encouragement from that, as well as from the fact that we share some common humanity with these folks.

Facing the Challenge

What, then, are specific things we can do to gain the upper hand with stage fright and to increase our effectiveness with an audience? Let's look at some steps which apply particularly to public speaking. Some of these points have obvious application to musical or dramatic performance as well.

   1. Staring fear down—revisited. Remember the perspective on fear that we discussed in chapter five? Part of what makes us leery about going into a situation where we might be afraid is the dread that fear may overwhelm us. We imagine that falling prey to stage fright is like tumbling headlong into a cavernous pit with no bottom; our fear will accelerate until it pushes us into a state of oblivion. In fact, stage fright is much less oppressive than all that. It always passes. It is not fatal. We can endure it, survive it and function within it much better than we probably imagine.

Indeed, with the right steps of control on your part, flashes of stage fright that occur once you are in front of an audience will usually be brief and not last for the duration of your presentation.

I personally find it helpful to take some deep breaths just before beginning a talk, following the technique suggested in chapter six. I make a conscious effort to relax my muscles and not clench my hands or jaw. These simple procedures bring quick results and always help deflate the onset of panic. Take control of your physical reactions to fear, and counteract them. Practice thought-stopping if necessary. These methods do work and will help to restore your sense of control.

Remember, too, the benefit of your analytical personality in facing a frightening situation such as giving a talk. You are not a represser. You have felt your fear and experienced it in depth before you ever set foot in front of the audience. This means you will not be *surprised* by the reaction of fear if it occurs. This fact alone will do much to rob fear of its grip on you. Stage fright in a public-speaking situation is much more intimidating when it comes on unexpectedly. The fact that you have anticipated it will make you less vulnerable to the panic cycle.

2. Don't be discouraged by past experiences. Many who are frightened of public speaking trace their fear to a traumatic childhood experience in front of an audience. You got up, confident and bubbly, to give a report in Mrs. Hill's English class but then blanked out. Mrs. Hill rebuked you for not being prepared, and classmates laughed at your debacle. Such experiences are common in childhood. Too often, though, they set in concrete for a lifetime our expectations about public-speaking situations. Remember that as an adult you now have gifts, knowledge and coping strategies which were not available to you as a child. *Your past does not have to define your future.*

Don't be deterred, either, if you have had an embarrassing experience in front of a group as an adult. You can learn from that experience and improve; you don't have to repeat the pattern. Even accomplished speakers report mortifying experiences in their early efforts to communicate to audiences. When Billy Graham became pastor of a church as a very young man, he prepared a series of four sermons to launch his ministry. On the first Sunday morning he was so nervous that he preached all four of them—in five minutes!

3. Pray for courage and effectiveness. Remember, too, the insights we stressed about the role of prayer in gaining victory over our fears. Set aside a specific period to thank God for the opportunity to give your presentation and to pray for strength, courage and articulateness as you give it. If you are facing a significant talk or one that is particularly challenging, allow thirty minutes to an hour for a time of concentrated prayer about it. And continue to ask God for help during your daily devotional time. Praying specifically for help in this way does wonders to open us to God's healing and empowerment.

4. Familiarize yourself with the setting. In getting ready for your presentation, give attention not only to preparing the content of your talk but to preparing yourself for the emotional experience of giving the talk. If you possibly can, visit the room where you will be speaking—when it is empty. Walk around it, familiarize yourself with it, stand on the stage or speaking area and visualize yourself speaking to the group. Even if you are quite familiar with the room, it can still help to make a visit there before anyone arrives, to make certain the setup is acceptable and remove any element of surprise. If unexpected changes have been made in the room arrangement, it is better to find out in advance than at the moment you walk in to give your talk, for then you have one less thing to adjust to.

5. *Preparing the setting*. Make sure a lectern is provided for you. It will give you a place to rest your arms and anchor your notes. If you have a choice, use the pulpit style lectern with a wide frame which conceals the lower part of your body. With your legs out of view of the audience, you will not need to be self-conscious about shaky knees. If a lectern is not present when you make your room check, make a point of asking someone in charge to find one. Don't simply assume it will show up when you give your talk. In churches, schools and professional auditoriums, lecterns and other speaking aids often have to be scouted out. Be certain the lectern is appropriate for your height; you should be able to rest your arms comfortably on it without stooping.

If you are giving a long presentation, you have a right to be assertive about the room setup. Don't assume that others will automatically arrange the chairs or tables in a way that is most conducive for communication. Those who set rooms usually default to stereotyped patterns which take little account of the speaker's or listeners' needs. From hundreds of lecture experiences in lots of different settings, I find that the room arrangement makes an enormous difference in my ability to communicate effectively and in the confidence I feel in front of an audience. I have often made or requested changes in the seating arrangement of a room to create a more personal environment. My preference is for chairs to be set in semicircles around the area where I'm speaking. And if the number of seats is under about 150, I opt for one large section of chairs with no aisles. While this makes it a bit more cumbersome for those finding a seat, it creates a more homogeneous and congenial setting for the lecture, which both the audience and I quickly feel.

If the room where you are speaking has movable chairs, it

takes only a few minutes to rearrange a setting of even several hundred seats. If you have any say over how the room is arranged, set the chairs in a way that gives you the greatest sense of personal contact with your audience as individuals. Talk with the person in charge of arrangements about your concern. Avoid a stilted room setup whenever possible.

6. *Live simulation helps.* If you have the freedom to do it, practice your talk once or twice in the room where you will actually give it. If you will be speaking with a public-address system, use it when you practice.

7. *Taming the microphone.* It's the little foxes that spoil the vines, and in the public-speaking situation the little fox is too often the microphone. Of course, in smaller audience situations you won't have a microphone to worry about. But when you do, it can make or break the initial confidence that you feel in front of an audience. When you step up to give your talk, the first thing you have to do is acclimate yourself to the microphone. Most inexperienced speakers do not anticipate this necessity and are thrown by it. Their awkwardness in adjusting to the mike increases their uneasiness and feeds their sense of panic. On the other hand, when you can adjust or don the mike quickly and professionally, you convey a sense of confidence to the audience and give your self-esteem a boost at the moment when you most need it.

If possible, practice working with the mike before giving your presentation. Learn its idiosyncrasies and remove the element of surprise; know exactly what you're doing. If you are dealing with a standing mike (on a floor stand or attached to the podium), keep several things in mind. Unless you preset it—and no one moves it in the meantime—you will almost certainly need to adjust its height before you speak. Almost all novice speakers make the mistake of not speaking closely enough to the mike. They assume that if it is within a foot or two of their mouth it will pick up their words. Most microphones, though, are designed to work best at close range. While you should not "kiss" the mike, you should make the effort to keep your mouth within two or three inches of the front of it. Adjust it so you can speak comfortably in that range, without having to lean toward it the whole time.

If the mike is on a goose-neck extension attached to the podium, simply bend it down or lift it up to the level of your mouth. If it is on a floor stand, however, you may have a greater challenge. Most speakers fail to anticipate how finicky microphone stands are to adjust. On many occasions I have watched a speaker struggle desperately to raise or lower a mike stand in front of a silent, waiting audience, only to finally give up and conclude the turning mechanism is broken. In most cases, though, the stand is just fine—the speaker just doesn't understand how it works. Most stands are designed with a top pole which fits inside a wider, lower pole; a turning gear allows you to adjust how far the top pole is pulled up out from the bottom. Most people grab the top pole and hold it tight while adjusting the turning gear. This is often a futile effort, especially if the gear has been overly tightened. The problem is that the gear is attached to the *bottom* pole, not the top. The solution, which usually works like a charm, is to grab the bottom pole while loosening the gear. Once it is loosened, quickly grab the top pole and pull it to the appropriate height, then tighten the gear. While this requires some extra gymnastics, with practice you can make the adjustment in seconds.

If you have a choice between a standing mike and a lapel mike, choose the lapel mike. Once it is donned, you don't have to worry about your distance from it when speaking. If you are using a wireless lapel mike, make sure you understand how to attach the transmission box to your belt and in which direction each of the tiny switches on the box must be set.

One of my first experiences with the wireless lavaliere occurred several years ago when I was guest preaching at a Presbyterian church. I thought I had attached the box correctly to my belt but apparently had not snapped it on tightly. Several minutes into my sermon, the box fell off my belt and dangled around my knees like an anchor, pulling on the microphone that was firmly attached to my tie. Since I was wearing a ministerial robe, no one knew this had happened. Because of the robe, there was no graceful way to reattach the box without disrupting the sanctity of the service. I decided to tolerate the inconvenience, though I felt as if I were being choked to death during the remainder of the message!

It's experiences like this that have taught me the importance of attending to the small details in getting ready for a talk. It can make a big difference in how comfortable you feel in front of an audience and often in your effectiveness as well.

8. Look your best. Do what you need to do to help yourself feel comfortable with your personal appearance in front of a crowd. Wear your best outfit. Get your hair cut or styled the way you most like it. This is no time to play Mr. or Ms. Humble. Take the time to look your best. The confidence you feel about your appearance will contribute to your overall sense of assurance while giving your presentation.

9. Don't let the acoustics throw you. There is a vast difference in acoustical ambience from room to room. You are especially likely to notice the difference if you are speaking over a public-address system. The placement of speakers around the room dramatically affects the way in which you hear your own voice coming back at you. In terms of what you expect to hear from the loudspeakers, be prepared for absolutely *anything.* In some rooms you scarcely hear your own voice over the sound system. In others it booms back to you. In some it encircles you like a warm blanket and adds to your personal sense of presence with the group. In others it echoes in the distance like amplified dispatches in a train station.

In most cases the audience can hear you just fine. What sounds unnatural to you sounds perfectly normal to them. They have been listening to others speaking over this system before you got up to speak and are used to its effects. And usually the sound system has been adjusted for the audience's benefit and not the speaker's; thus, what they hear is quite different from what hits your ears. The bottom line is, don't let those strange sounds coming from the loudspeaker—sounds that are supposed to be your voice—throw you. Unless you have clear reason to know there is a technical problem, assume that the audience is not being distracted and move on with your talk. Usually you do best not to comment on it, for the audience may not be able to understand what it is about the sound system that is bothering *you.*

Even if you do practice your talk over the public-address system beforehand, be aware that the acoustics can change dramatically when the room is full of people. The good news is that there is usually less echo with people present, and your voice will probably sound less eerie to you when the audience is there.

10. Preparation makes all the difference. Though it is beyond the scope of this book to give a full course in preparing an effective talk, let me make several suggestions about the preparation process which can help to boost your confidence.

If you are preparing for a lengthy, important talk, allow yourself a significant, leisurely time to prepare. Thirty minutes to an hour per one minute of lecture is a rule of thumb many accomplished speakers follow. Take the time you need to prepare your content, to "own" your material and to practice your delivery. As a general rule, the better rehearsed you are, the less nervous you will feel once you are on the front line.

Be certain that the main point of your talk is clear in your own mind and that you can express it equally clearly to your audience. In the first few minutes of your talk, state what that point is. And tell the audience how they will *benefit* from the information you will share with them. As you become confident you have material which will help them—and that they believe you do—your sense of purpose in giving this talk grows. This does wonders to calm the jitters.

Remember that in any single talk you cannot cover the waterfront on any topic; you can present only a few points effectively. Keep your points simple and clear. Realize that your purpose is not to educate your listeners fully on your subject but to whet their appetite for further learning. Knowing this takes pressure off you. Think of your role as a speaker in terms of the biblical metaphor of sowing seeds.

Wherever possible, be anecdotal rather than didactic in making your main points. Your audience will track with you better if you present your points in stories rather than straight lecture, and their attentiveness will encourage you. If you are speaking on a spiritual or personal theme, share from your own life as much as possible. Be vulnerable. Let them know you share their humanity. Your openness will foster a mutual sense of camaraderie, and that will help to decrease the anxiety you feel as well as help them learn better!

Give particular attention to the opening segment of your talk. If you get off to a good start in the first minute or two, you are likely to feel confident for your entire talk. Willard Scott notes that in preparing for his weather segments, "I make sure I know what my first line is going to be, even if it's something as simple as 'If you liked yesterday, you're going to love today' . . . so it doesn't surprise me or anybody else when it comes out of my mouth."[5]

In preparing my own talks, I sometimes spend as much time developing an attention-grabbing introduction as I do on the entire lecture itself. Ideally, I like to begin with a short, funny personal story which encapsulates the major point of the talk. These illustrations do not come naturally to me, and I have to allow time for coming up with them. Once I have chosen it, I will practice an opening anecdote fifteen or twenty times before giving an important talk. The result is that even if I am struck with stage fright when I first step up to the mike, I can run on automatic pilot until I recover. And the audience's positive reaction to the opening story spurs me on.

One further suggestion is to find a way to compliment your audience early on in your talk. Commend them for being present; thank them for taking the time to attend this event. And thank those who invited you by name. Let the audience perceive you as an affirming person; this will reverberate well in the way they respond to you.

11. Use visual aids. Remember that in dealing with phobic fear, any step that helps us focus on tangible reality draws our attention away from our fear and helps us cope. Focusing on the tangible details of giving your talk reduces your anxiety. This is why visual aids can be such a benefit. They not only help your audience better track with you, but they give you something to handle and fix your concentration on while you are speaking. If it is appropriate to the setting where you are speaking, use an overhead projector or blackboard and write out main points as you come to them. Use overhead transparencies or posters to help illustrate your points. If you are familiar with an area of multimedia technology, use it to your best advantage.

12. Body language revisited. Before I was to speak at a Christian singles meeting in Philadelphia, a young woman, Janet, sang several songs. Her voice was enjoyable, her style contemporary and her selection of songs good. Yet she looked ill at ease and had little eye contact with the audience. Predictably, the applause was polite but not zestful.

As she walked off stage she remarked to me, "They didn't smile!" She had expected a supportive cue from the audience. When it didn't come early in her performance, she thought the group didn't like her. From that point on her look of disappointment only made her acceptance more difficult. In reality, I think she expected too much too soon and underestimated how much the audience's response to her would be controlled by her own reactions. When I got up to speak, I found the group perfectly friendly and not at all the classic case of a hard audience. I'm certain there would have been plenty of smiles if Janet had simply been more affirming in her own facial responses to these people.

Keep in mind the points about body language which we stressed in chapter eleven, and apply them in the audience situation. Smile at your audience as much as possible. And look your audience in the eye. No matter how painful it feels to do so, no matter how devastating—even if you think the earth will open beneath you and swallow you up—*look these people in the eye.* And slowly move your glance around the audience as you speak. If folks are sitting on stage beside or behind you, glance at them too from time to time. Smiling and maintaining this sort of eye contact will produce reciprocal responses from audience members that will be reinforcing to you. And you will greatly increase your effectiveness in communicating.

13. Involve your audience! Unless you are speaking in a setting where it is simply inappropriate (a traditional worship service, a graduation ceremony), find ways to involve your audience. Let them do some of the work with you. As you anticipate your talk, you will be more relaxed if you know you have the audience-involvement time as a "safety valve." And any effort to involve them is likely to increase their attentiveness and appreciation for you as a speaker. Come up with a creative question or two on your topic which you can throw out for discussion in the early minutes of your talk. Entertain a half-dozen or so responses. The chemistry of this interaction with the audience can quickly vault you out of any initial panic you feel in facing the group.

Keep in mind the pointers about conversation which we stressed in chapter twelve, and apply these principles in responding to members of your audience. Find a way to affirm someone who answers a question or raises a point. Don't be argumentative with anyone during your presentation; unless you are uniquely skilled in the art of confrontation in a public setting (a Rush Limbaugh personality), it usually does not work well and you are likely to lose your train of thought. Put the accent on affirming your audience; err on the side of being an encourager. On the other hand, don't feel the compulsion to respond to every point or objection someone may raise. You are the speaker; you are in control and can decide what gets emphasized during this small window of time.

14. Revise your expectations. In the end, stage fright boils down to a problem of expectations, which goad us from two extremes: We expect the worst and demand perfection of ourselves at the same time. On the one hand, stage fright is a case of dreading the worst and dwelling on worst-case scenarios. We are possessed with thoughts like "I will fail miserably." "The audience will find me totally unappealing." "This fear will never end." We need to remind ourselves of what we have stressed—that the worst-case outcomes we dread seldom if ever occur. Remembering this can help stop this catastrophizing when it occurs. Remind yourself that there is a very low correlation between your worst-case fears and what actually transpires. Then use thought-stopping to halt your catastrophizing, and make a conscious effort to replace these fearful thoughts with more hopeful expectations.

At the same time, try not to be so hard on yourself in how you judge your effectiveness in a public-speaking situation. The truth is you do not need to be perfect—in fact, you do not need to be anywhere near perfect to be effective in relating to an audience. Even the most polished speakers make many mistakes and display plenty of humanness. In any audience situation, no matter how well you prepare, you will make mistakes and show your human side in many ways. Being human will actually help you relate more effectively to your audience, providing you can be *comfortable* being vulnerable.

Often what we fear most about the audience situation is that others will see the physical indications of our embarrassment—quivering lips, shaky knees, blushing face. Or we fear they'll detect our voice trembling. Again I want to emphasize the timeworn point stressed throughout this book, that these indications of shyness—if perceived at all—will work to your benefit if they are coupled with a proper degree of assertiveness and communication skill. As you make a reasonable effort to communicate with your audience, your human side will be endearing to them and will persuade them of your sincerity and earnestness. Don't be afraid of appearing human; and don't be afraid of coming off less than perfect.

At the same time, remember that others will probably not be nearly as conscious of these human factors or "imperfections" in your presentation as you are. There is a revealing passage of Scripture which brings this point home. Paul reflects on a visit to his friends in Corinth where, from his perception, his teaching and oratory were far from perfect:

> When I came to you, brothers, I did not come with eloquence or superior wisdom as I proclaimed to you the testimony about God. For I resolved to know nothing while I was with you except Jesus Christ and him crucified. I came to you in weakness and fear, and with much trembling. My message and my preaching were not with wise and persuasive words, but with a demonstration of the Spirit's power, so that your faith might not rest on men's wisdom, but on God's power. (1 Cor 2:1-5)

Two things are interesting about Paul's reflection. For one, he emphasizes that the humanity which he displayed in his presentations to these people, far from working against the effectiveness of his message, contributed to its power. In numerous ways God's strength shone through Paul's weakness. Paul was confident enough that he was not afraid to be weak.

But Paul was also one who by his very personality demanded perfection of himself. It is here that we gain an insight into this passage that is not evident on first glance. Consider the fact that we have no evidence that the Corinthians themselves actually perceived Paul as weak and stumbling and ineffective as a speaker. What is revealed in this passage is *Paul's* perception of how he came across; we are given a treasured window on his own self-image. All of the evidence we have suggests that others perceived Paul as a gifted, bold speaker. In the book of Acts, for instance, Luke writes the narrative, and in his many descriptions of Paul preaching and teaching there is not one instance where Paul comes off as suffering from a bad case of jitters. Through the eyes of one of his closest and most observant colleagues, Paul is depicted as a powerful personality in front of an audience.

I conclude that there was a distance between how Paul viewed himself and how others saw him. He was *much* more conscious of human factors and imperfections that were frankly not a problem from the standpoint of those in his audience. We can take encouragement from this reminder that others often see us in a more positive light than we see ourselves.

But even if humanness and imperfection are recognized, as Paul points out, they work for our advantage, increasing the impression of our sincerity and giving a unique channel for the Spirit of God to shine in our weakness. It is a *win-win* situation!

As you enter public-speaking situations, take heart. Give it your best effort. Pray earnestly that God will give you courage and effectiveness. But be comfortable with imperfection and with showing your human side. With this attitude you will be glorifying God through both your strength *and* your weakness. And that is what healthy spirituality and effective Christian living are all about.

Notes

Chapter One: A Common Experience
[1] Philip G. Zimbardo, *Shyness: What It Is, What to Do About It* (New York: Jove Books, 1977), pp. 25-26.
[2] Ibid., p. 28.
[3] Ibid., p. 41.

Chapter Two: The Roots of Shyness
[1] David V. Sheehan, *The Anxiety Disease* (New York: Bantam Books, 1983).
[2] Anne Moir and David Jessel, *Brain Sex: The Real Difference Between Men and Women* (New York: Lyle Stuart, 1991).

Chapter Three: The Benefits of Shyness
[1] John Calvin *Institutes of the Christian Religion* 3. 20. 2.
[2] Paul Tournier, *The Adventure of Living* (New York: Harper & Row, 1965).

Chapter Five: Staring Fear Down
[1] Manuel D. Zane and Harry Milt, *Your Phobia: Understanding Your Fears Through Contextual Therapy* (New York: Warner Books, 1984), p. 150.
[2] Ibid., pp. 140-41.
[3] Ibid., p. 150.
[4] Ibid., p. 154.
[5] Peter G. Hanson, *The Joy of Stress* (Kansas City, Mo.: Andrews, McMeel and Parker, 1985), pp. xix, 1-17.

Chapter Eight: Asking for Help
[1] Zane and Milt, *Your Phobia,* chaps. 8—9.
[2] Joan Guest, *Self-Esteem* (Downers Grove, Ill.: InterVarsity Press, 1984), p. 26.

Chapter Eleven: Warming Up to Conversation
[1]Carole Jackson, *Color Me Beautiful: Discover Your Natural Beauty Through the Colors That Make You Look Great and Feel Fabulous!* (New York: Ballantine, 1980); *Color for Men* (New York: Ballantine, 1984).

Chapter Twelve: Knowing What to Say
[1]Don Gabor, *How to Start a Conversation and Make Friends* (New York: Simon and Schuster, 1983), p. 42.
[2]M. Blaine Smith, *Should I Got Married?* (Downers Grove, Ill.: InterVarsity Press, 1990).
[3]Em Griffin, *Making Friends (& Making Them Count)* (Downers Grove, Ill.: InterVarsity Press, 1987).
[4]Joyce Huggett, *Dating, Sex and Friendship* (Downers Grove, Ill.: InterVarsity Press, 1985).

Chapter Thirteen: Faith and Assertiveness
[1]Manuel J. Smith, *When I Say No, I Feel Guilty* (New York: Dial Press, 1975).
[2]Omar K. Omland, *The Third Mile: A Biblical View of Codependency* (Fergus Falls, Minn.: Faith and Fellowship Press, 1992).

Chapter Fifteen: Learning Optimism
[1]Paul Tournier, *The Adventure of Living* (New York: Harper & Row, 1965), p. 127.
[2]Thomas J. Peters and Robert H. Waterman Jr., *In Search of Excellence: Lessons from America's Best-Run Companies* (New York: Warner Books, 1982), pp. 141-42, 210-11.

Chapter Sixteen: Playing a Role—and Staying Whole
[1]Joan C. Harvey with Cynthia Katz, *If I'm So Successful, Why Do I Feel like a Fake? The Impostor Phenomenon* (New York: St. Martin's Press, 1985).
[2]Paul Tournier, *The Meaning of Persons* (New York: Harper & Row, 1957).
[3]Ibid., pp. 69, 80.
[4]Ibid., p. 78.

Appendix
[1]David Sharp, "Send in the Crowds," *Health Magazine* 6 (April 1992): 66.
[2]Ibid., pp. 66-67.
[3]Ibid., p. 66.
[4]Ibid., p. 70.
[5]Ibid.

About the Author

Blaine Smith, a Presbyterian pastor, is director of Nehemiah Ministries, a resource ministry based in the Washington, D.C., area. His work includes giving seminars, lectures and conferences, counseling and writing. He is author of *Knowing God's Will*, *Should I Get Married?* and *One of a Kind* as well as numerous articles. He is also the lecturer for "Guidance By The Book," a home study course with audio cassettes produced by the Christian Broadcasting Network as part of its Living By The Book series.

Blaine is a graduate of Georgetown University and holds a Master of Divinity degree from Wesley Theological Seminary and a Doctor of Ministry degree from Fuller Theological Seminary. He lives in Damascus, Maryland, with his wife, Evie, and their two sons, Benjamin and Nathan.

You Can Receive Blaine's Newsletter

Blaine authors a monthly newsletter, *Nehemiah Notes*. It includes an article each month on topics related to realizing your potential in Christ and keeping a grace-centered perspective in the Christian life. It is sent free to anyone requesting it.

To request the newsletter or correspond with Blaine, you may write:

Nehemiah Ministries
P.O. Box 448
Damascus, MD 20872